KEYS TO STARTING AND OWNING A BUSINESS

By
Carole Sinclair

BARRON'S

© Copyright 1991 by Carole Sinclair

All right reserved.
No part of this book may be reproduced in any form,
by photostat, microfilm, xerography, or any other
information retrieval system, electronic or mechanical,
without the written permission of the copyright owner.

All inquiries should be addressed to:
Barron's Educational Series, Inc.
250 Wireless Boulevard
Hauppauge, NY 11788

Library of Congress Catalog Card Number 90–25242

International Standard Book Number 0-8120-4609-9

Library of Congress Cataloging-in-Publication Data

Sinclair, Carole.
    Keys for women starting and owning a business / by Carole Sinclair.
       p.   cm. – (Barron's business keys)
    Includes index.
    ISBN 0-8120-4609-9
    1. New business enterprises.   2. Women in business.   I. Title.
II. Series.
  HD62.5.S57   1991
  658.1'1'082–dc20   90-25242
                                                                                        CIP

PRINTED IN THE UNITED STATES OF AMERICA

4   5500   98765432

DEDICATION

This book is dedicated to Sylvia Porter, my longtime business partner and friend

ACKNOWLEDGMENTS

I wish to acknowledge first, the inspiration of Sylvia Porter; Caroline Urbas, my managing editor and sounding board; Alan Hartnick, for his legal advice; DeWitt Stern, for his insurance advice; and finally my daughter, Wendy, for her everyday warmth and support.

TO THE READER

This book is intended to provide general information. The publisher, authors and copyright owner are not engaged in rendering personal finance, investment, tax, accounting, legal, or other professional advice and services and cannot assume responsibility for individual decisions made by readers.

Should assistance for these types of advice and services be required, professionals should be consulted.

References to tax provisions in this book are based on current tax laws and regulations. Revisions in tax law, if adopted, might affect the tax consequences.

CONTENTS

Introduction vii

1. Where Female Entrepreneurs Come from 1
2. Who Are the Successful Female Entrepreneurs? 3
3. Will You Be Happy if You Start a Business? 4
4. Why Do Businesses Fail? 7
5. Preparation for the Business Owner 9
6. Entrepreneurs Sell 11
7. What Kind of Business? 13
8. Half-Way Steps 15
9. Servicing a Former Employer 16
10. Becoming a Consultant 18
11. Expanding a Side Business 20
12. Buying an Existing Business 21
13. The Franchise Route 23
14. Selling to the Government 25
15. Dealing With Foreign Businesses 26
16. Look to Your Future 28
17. The Time and the Place 29
18. Time Management 31
19. The Feasibility Study 32
20. The Business Plan 34
21. Business Organization 36
22. Naming Your Company 39
23. Legal Matters 40
24. Assistance and Information 42
25. Raising Money 44
26. Cash Requirements Early On 46
27. Financing the Ongoing Operation 48
28. What to Do if the Money Runs Out 50
29. Personal Cash 51
30. Savings and Inflation 53

31 Cash Flow 55
32 Taxes, Taxes, Taxes 58
33 Discrimination 59
34 Multiple Businesses 61
35 Learning to Delegate 62
36 Maintaining a Company Mailing List 63
37 Travel and Entertainment 64
38 The Office 66
39 Staff 69
40 Personnel Matters 71
41 Hiring Family Members 75
42 Summer or Seasonal Interns 77
43 Bringing in Management Talent 78
44 Personnel Problems 80
45 Seeking the Help of Professionals 82
46 Insurance 84
47 Projecting a Positive Image 87
48 Marketing 89
49 Problems 93
50 Paying Back Your Community 96
51 The Role of the Owner 97
52 Selling Your Company 99
53 Some Case Histories 101

Appendices
   1 Sample Feasibility Study 106
   2 Assessing the Feasibility Study 109
   3 The Business Plan 111
   4 Job Descriptions 114
   5 Preparing Your Personal Net Worth Statement 120
   6 Maintaining a Positive Personal Cash Flow 122

Questions and Answers 124
Glossary 128
Index 131

INTRODUCTION

A generation ago, many women could look forward to a relatively stable life. They married early, had children, stayed married, and their working husbands retired with pensions and lifetime healthcare benefits. Although most of these women ultimately became widows, their basic financial needs were taken care of.

Women now live in an extremely unstable condition. Many of them still marry young, but half of them divorce. Among those who stay married, many of their husbands are laid off or downsized, pensions disappear, and health benefits disappear or get cut way back. In addition to the burden and cost of raising children, many of these women now face the responsibility of caring for aging parents at the same time. Women are expected to be wives, employees, mothers, and caretakers all at once with no certainty of job security or retirement and health benefits in later life.

It is not surprising that many women have concluded that they had better get their financial lives under control, and many of them feel that the best way to do it is to have their own businesses where they can control the time, investment, and payment.

You've decided you'd like to start your own business. The first question you should ask yourself is, "What kind of business do I want to start?" It is essential that it be something you know a great deal about, perhaps something you've done while employed for others or something you've done as a hobby.

Make an effort to determine if you are the type who is likely to succeed in an entrepreneurial pursuit. Do you work well alone? Can you handle a lot of emotional stress and trouble and pressure? Are you organized? Are you disciplined? Are you prepared for the long haul? Are you prepared to work long hours, possibly seven days a week? If you are not answering yes to most or all of these questions, you should rethink whether a venture in entrepreneurism is for you.

Is it possible to start your business on the side? You'll have minimal risk if you keep your full-time job while launching your business on the side so that if it does not work out as planned, your income stream is not interrupted or terminated.

You will need to be able to answer these questions:

Is there an actual need for the service or product your company is going to provide or make? What do you know about the competition? Who will your market be? How are you going to reach your market?

If at all possible, try to launch your business with your own capital and at your own location. There are tremendous advantages to testing your business concepts with a very small investment, out of your home.

1

WHERE FEMALE ENTREPRENEURS COME FROM

The status of women employed in corporations is interestingly a lot like the status of men. Both are experiencing insecurity, downsizing, layoffs, and an increasing need for further technological education. The women now entering the workforce are educated like men, hired like men and appear to be promoted—as well as fired—like men.

Ahead of them in the corporations, however, is the original generation of women to enter the workforce after major changes in women's rights in the 1960s. These women were not educated like men, were not hired and promoted like men, and it is from this very large group that significant numbers of female entrepreneurs are drawn. These women in some cases hit what is called the "glass ceiling," an invisible barrier keeping them from the top corporate positions.

In many cases, these women have the classic entrepreneurial traits of independence, competitiveness, aggressiveness, ability to work alone, discipline, and comfort with a high risk level. Many of these women have benefited from their years in the corporation and received substantial training in a number of areas including sales and marketing, new product development, or accounting and finance. With these qualifications, as well as an in-depth knowledge of a particular industry and the motivation of having hit a seemingly dead end, these relatively high-powered women go out on their own.

A second group of women who start their own businesses are those who had a formal education or at least a partial formal education before marrying and raising children. These women opt to start a small business of their own rather than enter the corporate workforce, generally looking for flexible hours and part-time work. Many of these women convert a hobby or personal interest into a small company.

A third group of women starting their own businesses is composed of retired women or women who were involuntarily retired early. Some of these women face the unusual prospect of being retired more years than they were gainfully employed and lack the financial resources to withdraw from the workforce. When these women have been associated with one company all of their working lives, switching to another corporation is not appealing, and they make the move on to their own out of unexpected financial necessity. These women are just like their male counterparts, caught in the same sort of situation.

2
WHO ARE THE SUCCESSFUL FEMALE ENTREPRENEURS?

They come from the same pool as do successful male entrepreneurs. Most of these women are from middle class or working class backgrounds. Many of them are the first in their families to go to college. Like their male counterparts, many of these women are the oldest child in their families. They tend not to have gone to elite schools. Most of them in some way worked their way through college, and most of them had some sort of scholarship help. They, like their male counterparts, succeeded on motivation.

Approximately thirty percent of all businesses in the United States are owned by women. However, women-owned businesses are growing at four times the rate of male-owned businesses.

The outlook for female entrepreneurs is excellent.

The United States business world faces international economic competition as well as a coming shortage of skilled labor. Corporations will have trouble finding and keeping top flight people. Increasingly they will look to small businesses for services and products they might have generated internally in the past.

3

WILL YOU BE HAPPY IF YOU START A BUSINESS?

You need to give serious thought as to whether you are independent or like company. Are you resourceful on your own, or do you gain your motivation from groups? Are you a loner or are you a team player? Do you like to take risks? Do you bounce back? Do you like to sell? Has your job, career, or work been central to your existence in the past? Do you want it to be in the future? Is financial security critical to you?

You need to spend time thinking about or possibly talking about what your life will be like if you start your own business. You might have a great idea for a product or service and know your market very well, but unless you find a challenge invigorating, you could be rendered ineffective by being perpetually on your own, out on a limb.

Risk tolerance. It's important to assess the amount of risk with which you are comfortable. If you are conservative, do not like unnecessary risk and feel more comfortable when there is a certainty, you will not enjoy having a business of your own.

You might enjoy a partnership with someone who has been established and has a track record, where you become a part of the operation in exchange for a piece of the bottom line in a business that has been in existence for a number of years. If, on the other hand, you genuinely enjoy taking risks, you will probably enjoy the process of starting and trying your own business and if successful, may even find yourself selling your business and moving on to start another one because it is the risk element you enjoy the most.

Are You the Entrepreneurial Type?

1. Are you optimistic?
2. Do you have a high energy level?
3. Would you define yourself as a workaholic?
4. Do you like to work alone?
5. Are you used to relying on your wits to get by, or do you need a strong support system?
6. Do you like to take risks?
7. Are you creative?
8. Do you constantly spot opportunities that other people miss?
9. Are you organized?
10. Are you disciplined?
11. Do you like to sell . . . yourself or your business?
12. Do you have the family freedom to radically change your life, or are there a number of people who are dependent on you for stability, income, time?
13. Do you bounce back quickly from disappointments?
14. Can you develop and defend your position on important matters?
15. Are you good with people? Are you comfortable hiring and supervising different types of employees?
16. Do you require an even keel and a stable existence, or are you game for a little danger and adventure?
17. Are you self reliant?
18. Is your self esteem a result of your own analysis or that of others?
19. Do you have the patience to persuade others to your way of thinking?
20. Can you build excitement and enthusiasm in others?
21. Can you motivate others?

22. Can you, if things don't work out, cut your losses and walk away from something without dwelling on the past?
23. Do you want to be your own boss?
24. Have you seized every available career opportunity to learn from others and to absorb their strategies?
25. Can you take any business idea and quickly assess its positive and negative points?
26. Can you get directly to the heart of the marketability of a business idea?
27. Can you focus on the core of a concept and move quickly to the important points?
28. Do you enjoy speaking publicly?
29. Do you enjoy writing about your field?
30. Do you like competition and do you like a good fight?
31. Have you made some provision for your future, your retirement, and your dependents?
32. Can you set aside liquid assets equal to three to six months', or better yet a year's worth of expenses?
33. Can you appreciate the good ideas of others and not feel threatened by them?
34. Do you always make a point of giving others credit for their work?
35. Is independence a major priority for you?

If you've answered yes to more than three quarters of these questions, you are the classic entrepreneurial type. If you attempt a business startup, it will probably bring you happiness, whether or not it brings you wealth.

If on the other hand, your response to most of these questions was negative, entrepreneurism is not for you. It will cause you too much stress, instability, and anxiety. It's not worth it.

4

WHY DO BUSINESSES FAIL?

Female-owned and male-owned businesses fail at about the same rate and always for the same reasons. The main reason is that the small start-up businesses are under-capitalized. As we discuss elsewhere in the book, cash flow projections must be conservative and must be made for a minimum of three years before any business launch.

Entrepreneurs tend to be optimistic. A good balance to the entrepreneur is the banker and the accountant, familiar with new business startups, who will bring the figures back to reality.

The second major reason for business failures is that the entrepreneur lacks management ability. I stress later on (see Key 6) the importance of using your corporate life, if there has been corporate life before the entrepreneurial venture, to get experience in sales, budget management, and staff supervision. Without these bases covered, the entrepreneur must bring in the necessary management talent. Since a major motivation of all entrepreneurs is to run the show, it can be difficult for the entrepreneur to face the fact that she may be the creative force but needs to bring in administrative and sales experience.

Another common pitfall is the inability of the entrepreneur to face up to the need for experienced management once the business begins to grow. The owner may read the business growth as a vote of personal approval of the way she runs the company. That may be true, up to a point, but there is a great difference between managing a company of ten or fewer employees and one of fifty or more.

The board of advisors (see Key 44) provides an excellent sounding board for monitoring both management and financial needs of a growing young company. Be sure to draw on the expertise of these people frequently.

Be honest about where your own strengths lie. Do not get yourself involved in a business that does not tap your real strengths, but requires those you do not have and do not wish to bring in from the outside.

In addition to all the other information you need to amass before actually starting a business, you should make yourself familiar with the failure rate of small businesses in your category and in your geographical location. Check these figures out with the Small Business Administration, the local chapter of your trade organization, and your local Chamber of Commerce. If there is a pattern to the failures, ascertain what it is and avoid falling into this trap yourself. You will most likely discover that business failures in your area of interest are attributable to a lack of capital and lack of management experience on the part of the principal or principals of the business.

5

PREPARATION FOR THE BUSINESS OWNER

Women who start their own businesses after moving through the corporate ranks generally do not need any special training in supervising and hiring staff. Women who have basically been at home, accustomed to dealing only with children and perhaps repairmen and domestics, may in fact need training to help them bring out their special skills in dealing with people, supervising people, hiring and firing people, and generally taking charge.

Women who have organized and run school activities, religious activities, and charitable activities have gotten more than their share of experience in organizing, budgeting, and delegating, but frequently these very same women do not place the proper value on this experience and need to be reminded of their past achievements.

Management and assertiveness seminars can be very useful here. These are often offered by local colleges and by women's organizations.

Consider additional training or education in specific areas required by your new business. If you already have a college degree, you might decide to take additional courses in computer literacy, accounting, financial planning, design, whatever is appropriate. Local and community colleges are one possibility. In addition, trade organizations in your field probably sponsor educational events. Correspondence courses, which vary greatly in quality, are also a potential source of training.

Attending "how to" seminars in your field is always a good idea because in addition to providing periodic refresher courses in your area, they provide excellent opportunities for networking with other people who work in your field. (See Key 46.)

6
ENTREPRENEURS SELL

The main thing you will do as an entrepreneur is sell. You'll be first of all selling yourself to suppliers, customers, investors. Second, you'll be selling your product or service. And third, you'll be selling the advantages to employees, suppliers, and customers of your small business versus a larger, well-established competitor. Selling is extremely hard and requires that you force yourself to be "up" most of the time. This does take its toll, if not on the job, then off the job. Some people thrive on the "high" of selling and closing a sale, and somehow cope with the accompanying down when things don't work out. Others find the whole emotional swing devastating, and they would be best advised not to become entrepreneurs.

Sales experience. I personally feel that if at this point you have no sales experience—experience selling something directly—you should get it. It is unlikely that a lending institution will be interested in lending you money unless you can show that you have the ability to sell your service or product and have some related experience. If, on the other hand, you are the creative force and you have a partner with sales and business experience, the combination should be effective in your presentation of your business plan to the lending institution.

Corporate experience. If you are currently in a corporation in a non-sales capacity and you have never had sales experience, you should consider seeking a transfer to some sales department. If in your mind you know you're going to start your own business in six months or a year or two years, the best possible training you could give yourself while enjoying the salary and full benefits at your corporation would be first-person experience in sales. You need to know how to present your product, develop a sales presentation with historical data and future projections, and a competitive analysis. Finally, you need to know how to close a sale. It may seem like a formidable task if you have never been involved in such an operation, but actually anyone can do it. It's a matter of being clear in your objective, focused, determined.

Since you are planning to start your own business, you must know how to make your client or customer want the service or product you have available. You must know how to sell its benefits. You must learn the all-important trick of understanding the needs of your client or customer *first* so that you can customize each and every sales pitch to the very specific needs of the customers.

It is possible to receive this training at your own expense in various commercial programs. But why do that? It makes a lot more sense for you to hold on to your secure benefits and salary while learning this skill and producing a result for your employer.

7

WHAT KIND OF BUSINESS?

If you have a strong entrepreneurial urge but have no particular business in mind, the best advice is to look at projections for growth over the next ten or twenty years. You might simply check newspaper headlines for the last six months or a year to see what businesses mirror major changes in our world. For instance, as the population ages, health care and products that meet the needs of older people are experiencing and will continue to experience enormous growth. Even though the housing market is currently in a slump, housing for seniors is booming.

As the economy becomes less national and more global, a proficiency in languages is extremely desirable and products and services that assist in development of these language skills can be expected to sell.

The environment has become a major political issue in the United States. Businesses dealing in waste management, and all kinds of environmental preservation should fare well. The list could go on.

Conversely, if the population is aging, services for children will be in less demand. Each of the growth areas has a flip side which should be avoided.

Know your field. Stick with something you know and understand. Your chances of succeeding in your own business, like your chances of succeeding in the stockmarket, are many, many times greater if you are knowledgeable in depth in the area. This is not the time to take a flyer.

Quality. Whatever your business, quality should be your number one goal. It is a mistake to try to be fast, cheap, cut corners, or simply knock off the competition.

In order for you to succeed in any meaningful way, you must produce something distinctive, of the very highest quality possible. A quality operation, even when small, attracts first-rate employees as well as customers. Banks like doing business with quality operations, even small ones.

Services versus products. Most of this book makes the assumption that your business will likely be a service business where you provide your service to the ultimate consumer. More than half the businesses owned by women are service businesses. You may, however, decide to have a product business. You might manufacture the product, or service the middle man or wholesaler between the manufacturer and retailers, or you might open a retail establishment to sell products.

Of these options manufacturing is, of course, the most difficult. It requires raw materials, equipment, inventories, and complex dealings with wholesalers and retailers.

Wholesaling might appear on the surface to be the easiest of the three in that you don't have to manufacture anything—you take someone else's manufactured product and sell it to retailers. But the truth is that wholesaling is complex and profit margins in the middle are slim and require lots of volume. You also need to know both ends of the business. You need to know manufacturers and the manufacturing process and you need to know the retail outlets and their requirements.

Opening a retail establishment holds a great deal of appeal for many people. On the surface it looks not difficult to establish a business where you sell food, or flowers, or whatever. The biggest difficulty is not in acquiring the goods. It is more likely to be the difficulty in getting your customers to pay. This will cause you an immediate cash flow difficulty. Changing neighborhoods and traffic patterns are another headache. Competitors who appear overnight are yet another difficult matter to deal with.

Be aware of the likely difficulties before you embark on your enterprise.

8

HALF-WAY STEPS

In addition to the possibility of your providing a service or product on your own, there are other options open to you. You might try "intrapreneuring" if you have a particularly enlightened employer anxious to compensate the best employees. You might be able to work out an arrangement where you develop a product or service while employed, with full salary and benefits, and then receive "a piece of the action" from your service or product once your employer pays all of the costs to launch it.

Freelance sales. Whatever your interests, it is probably possible for you to arrange to sell a related product, on a commission basis, for someone else's operation. Such arrangements are common in real estate. While you may have to put forth some effort and time to gain the appropriate license or certification, it is possible to gain experience and begin to build a list of clients while working part time on a commission basis for someone else. When you sense that you have learned a lot about the business, it might be time to make your move. This would put you in a position where you might be competing directly with your former associate, but in areas such as real estate, brokers come to expect a lot of turnover.

9
SERVICING A FORMER EMPLOYER

American corporations are downsizing, slashing budgets, eliminating certain optional services as they strive to be competitive in a world market. If you have been downsized, a possible business for you is one that provides the service that you used to provide for a former employer. For instance, one of the first departments cut during any budget tightening is public relations. This may be a good or bad idea, but since public relations effects can rarely be measured, it's always a vulnerable department. Let's say you ran this department or were a senior person in it at your company and that department cost your employer $100,000 a year. You might consider establishing your own public relations operation at home, with minimal costs, and proposing to your former employer that you provide the services for say $25,000 a year. For the company, it's a huge savings while permitting them to maintain some public relations presence. For you, it's an ideal first client, bringing in a reliable source of income while you search for other clients. It also gives you an immediate portfolio item to use in courting other clients. This is the sort of deal best worked out before you leave the company.

Another possibility is in the R&D area. Let's say you worked in your corporation's research and development and you were working on a promising new product for your company. When cuts had to be made, your area was cut. You might approach your former employer and, for a small reasonable fee, agree to continue development of the product on your own. You might propose that if you develop it and patent it, you and your corporation will share in the profits from the development and distribution. Your corporation still gets the competitive new product, you still get to work on something you have devoted time and energy to, and both of you share in profits.

Your responsibility to your former employer. If you had any written agreement with any former employer regarding the issue of non-compete, it is wise to have this reviewed by your attorney before establishing your new business. For instance, if you were working on a secret new software project for a former employer and you start a software business that produces a strikingly similar item, having signed a non-compete agreement with your former employer could put you in serious legal trouble. It is essential to go back and review agreements that were signed even many, many years ago.

10

BECOMING A CONSULTANT

Life as a consultant seems to have everything going for it. First of all, all you need is a business card, letterhead, and a phone to get started. Since most consulting is done on the premises of the client, office space is not essential. A consulting business can be run from the living room or dining room. Presumably you are something of an authority on something. Whatever that is qualifies you as a consultant in that area. Of course, if you have had paid, senior positions in a given area, that will allow you to be a somewhat more authoritative consultant. Consulting, indeed, has everything going for it, everything but predictable cash flow—or any cash flow at all.

The easiest way to become a consultant is to call people you know who you think will benefit from your expertise in your given area. Once you get one or two clients in this fashion, you will find that your business will grow primarily through word of mouth. Most consultants do not advertise. Consultants are in demand when it is known in a particular field that they have advised so and so who then, based on that advice, took certain steps that led to success and profit. Established consultants, of course, have office space and, in some cases, vast staffs.

The advantage of being a consultant is that you instantly have your own business, presumably some income, and hours of your choosing. On the other hand, consulting involves what are called "cold calls." These are very hard to make. They involve making sales pitches, generally on the phone, followed by a letter, which makes another kind of pitch, followed, if you're lucky, with a face-to-face meeting in which you will attempt to close the sale. For some consultants, one out of ten or twenty or thirty such pitches results in a client. Selling yourself and your service is the key here to success.

Because of its nature, this is certainly the kind of business it is possible to quietly get going on the side. Such businesses are best launched from the safety of a dependable paycheck. Under certain circumstances, like early retirement, it might even be appropriate for you to consult for your former employer—the absolute best arrangement possible.

If you have been "downsized" at your corporation and your parting is friendly and has nothing to do with your performance on the job, do everything you can to get even a short-term consulting contract from your employer. It is an ideal situation if you can provide your service or product to your former employer for six months or a year while you get your feet on the ground in your business. A former employer is also an ideal reference for banks, insurance companies, etc.

11
EXPANDING A SIDE BUSINESS

If you start a business on the side and it is thriving and you're doing well financially, out of your home, with no significant investment, it does not necessarily follow that if you were to quit your job and do it full time that you would double or triple your business. Some small businesses should be small; there's a limited though lucrative market that does not take eight hours a day to service. Don't make the mistake of being romantic about the idea of expansion. In some cases it's a terrible mistake—you lose the income from a regular job, the corporate benefits including possibly health benefits and a pension, and you end up with real estate and equipment leases and debt that you cannot justify in terms of sales.

If you are in a situation with a very successful business, seek the advice of professionals before you consider expanding without cause.

12

BUYING AN EXISTING BUSINESS

Another option open to you is buying an existing business. If you do this, it is essential to bring in outside experts to assess this company. You will need the services of an accounting firm, a law firm, and a bank. Do not try to make an emotional determination on your own because you like the product or the current owner, etc. This is a case where someone needs to look at the numbers with a cold eye. Why is the current owner selling? Has the business begun to fail or slow down? Is there serious new competition?

Finding a business. If you have decided that your preference is to buy an ongoing business, you can pursue this either on your own or with the help of experts. If you pursue it on your own, you can consult the business opportunities sections of newspapers and magazines. You can visit trade organizations that act as clearinghouses for such opportunities, or you can seek help through a bank or brokerage firm or other lending institution. All of these operations will put you together with business owners who want to sell and they will take a fee, when the transaction is completed, for their services. If the group simply finds the business for you, the fee will be somewhat lower than if they find the business, analyze it, and arrange the financing for you to purchase it. Review any proposals from any of these groups with your attorney, banker, and accountant.

What you should look for in an ongoing business purchase.
- Does the firm have excellent management in all areas, or is it dominated by an owner with expertise in only one area?

- Has there been a substantial investment in research and development?
- Are the products or services of the firm being constantly adapted to the ever-changing marketplace in an effort to stay competitive?
- Does the purchase price reflect the current health of the company and its likely future growth, or does it reflect a past success? You need to consult with your banker, lawyer, and accountant regarding the asking price and an appropriate offer you can make based on documented future projections.
- Are you going to buy the business outright or are you going to buy *into* the business (a small piece right now) with the option to buy more or all of it at a predetermined date and price? The advantage of buying only a piece going in is that you get to live with the business, analyze the business, and compare the revenue and expense projections against actuals while you are involved in the business.

Financing terms. Whether you are buying part or all of the business, are the terms favorable to you? You should aim for the smallest possible down payment and the longest possible payout with the smallest possible installment at the lowest possible interest. The seller is of course interested in just the reverse. It's important to calculate the current value of money when working out your purchase terms. Again, seek the advice of your accountant and lawyer, especially regarding the tax ramifications of various methods of financing the business.

You will want a non-compete clause from the current seller so that he cannot turn around and start up the very same kind of business competing with you, putting you at a terrific disadvantage since he will know the inside details of your business.

13

THE FRANCHISE ROUTE

If, after study, you have decided that you want your own business but don't want to be totally alone with a startup, you may decide that a franchise is the answer. And perhaps it is. Your first step is to consult a lawyer who will help you review the documents that franchisors are required to provide to interested franchisees. These will include a description of the current status of the business, a history of the business, a profile of the management of the company, previous profit and loss statements, and projected profits and losses for one to three years.

This information should also include a very detailed description of exactly what the franchisor is willing to do for you. There is a great range of possibilities, starting with simply lending you the name and leaving you on your own for the rest. A more likely scenario, however, is that the franchise in which you are interested already has a number of branches. Most probably, they have a uniform look, similar kind of location and space, and a detailed written marketing guide regarding how to produce and/or sell the product or service. Some even require that locations be exact duplicates, that staff wear a uniform, and that production codes be strictly adhered to. You might also find that the franchisor takes sole responsibility for advertising and promotion. In such a scenario, you would be the owner/manager of the franchise. It would be up to you to watch the operation carefully, motivate your employees, satisfy your customers, and put in the long hours necessary to establish your location. Perhaps the franchisor even selects the site for you. This can be a blessing, since many franchisee's starting out make the mistake of selecting a cheap location rather than one that's a good buy for the money, in a high-traffic growth area, with not too much competition nearby.

As you might expect, the franchisor providing the most guidance, marketing services, etc., takes the biggest piece of the income that you generate. In return, you get to become part of an ongoing successful business chain with little risk to you.

Another scenario, at the opposite end of the spectrum, is one where you pay the franchisor a lump sum up front and take your chances, trying to duplicate the success of the original franchise. This can be risky and dangerous and opens up the possibility of fraud if the agreement is not properly reviewed by your attorney. If your goal is not to get rich but to earn a comfortable income and be on your own while experiencing little or no financial risk or investment, a well-established franchise might be just the thing for you.

14

SELLING TO THE GOVERNMENT

All governments are required to go through elaborate procedures and to seek multiple bids before contracting out for any kind of product or service. Government contracts can be tremendously lucrative once established. If your product or service is of any interest to your local, state, or federal government, by all means devote the time to learning how to bid on these contracts. The process is always intricate and time consuming. You may not win the contract the first time, but you will have gained important experience. These contracts are worth pursuing even if your profit margin is small in the beginning as they can help to build volume for your company that will make it possible for you to ultimately produce your products or services at a lower unit cost.

15

DEALING WITH FOREIGN BUSINESSES

Your business may require that you deal with foreign businesses, either as clients, customers, or suppliers. You will learn what the men before you learned, namely that many foreign cultures are very different from ours. One of the most striking differences, especially in underdeveloped countries, is the treatment of women and the general status of women. You have to do your best to operate as a business owner, rather than as a woman, or a wife. This can test your patience and endurance, but if your goal is to do business with a foreign country whose culture offends you, you will have to decide either not to deal with them or accept their attitudes.

Women in the United States live in probably the most prejudice-free, wide-open, liberated business atmosphere for women. Things are not perfect here, and there is certainly lots of room for improvement, but the situation abroad in certain parts of the world is similar to the atmosphere here twenty-five, fifty or even a hundred years ago.

Before attempting any business investment (of your time or money) abroad, you should seek the advice of a professional (banker, accountant, lawyer, consultant) who has had in-depth experience in the country in which you are interested.

Cultural and religious roadblocks include countries where women are forbidden to own a company, forbidden to appear in public places necessary for execution of their business, forbidden from appearing at all without their heads and arms and legs fully covered, forbidden from any entry to the kinds of private clubs (social and sports activity) where so much business is conducted.

In some of these cases, there are laws forbidding this behavior and in other places it is simply strongly discouraged by the existing culture.

As you can imagine, it is probably simply impossible to have a business dealing with any country where, for instance, women are considered the property of their fathers and then husbands. Until the women in these countries achieve their own satisfactory status and liberation in their business communities, it is extraordinarily difficult for American women to come in and make any significant inroads.

In other countries, it would simply be impossible to find male staff for any kind of operation you might want to set up, and in those countries, generally, the women don't work at all in business.

16
LOOK TO YOUR FUTURE

As you make your exciting plans for your new business, remember that the economic times ahead will be different. The United States will experience a shortage of skilled workers. If your business will employ highly skilled technical workers, be prepared to pay top price.

Chances are, you will live much longer than your parents or grandparents. If you take early retirement from your corporation in your forties or fifties, you will need to support yourself from the proceeds of your new business for perhaps thirty or forty years.

The value of your home could remain flat or even decline as the next generation has fewer buyers. Your parents' generation may have funded their retirement by selling the family home. You will probably not be able to do that.

Health care costs are out of control. One reasonable reaction to this is a new interest in preventative measures. Be sure that your business does not "feed" old living habits that will be out of vogue in the next couple of years.

Since it is likely that your new business will finance the second half of your life, be certain that it's in an area where you will be happy at that age—with the location, the service or product, the customers or clients, the necessary travel, personal appearances, etc.

17

THE TIME AND PLACE

When is the time to start your own business? This is a complicated question. But what it comes down to is that it's the right time when it is your best option and a viable option. In other words, if the business is feasible (see Key 19), and economically, professionally, and personally starting a business is a good option for you, then it's the right time.

Ideally, you will start your own business after spending several years in your field of interest, where you will have benefited from experience in a larger successful corporation. Your experience will have covered product or service development, sales, and management. You will have had experience supervising people at various levels and bottom-line experience for the budget of a department or a division as well as hands-on experience selling your product or service.

But the ideal may be impossible for you, and waiting for the perfect time may mean that you never start. Women who wait until their children are a certain age or have gone off to school are frequently trapped unexpectedly by another time-consuming difficulty such as the care of aging parents or relatives, a divorce, or a husband whose career has been terminated by a layoff, downsizing, or health difficulty.

Location. You may have concluded that since you have made the tough decision to leave the safety of an employer for your own business, you might as well establish your business in some interesting new location. This is probably a mistake. Starting your own business is fraught with enough potential pitfalls without adding to it the prospect of an entirely new community and/or state. During the year or years when your business is starting out, you will need to take comfort in as much as possible that is familiar. It could be a serious mistake to try to establish a business where you are unfamiliar with the population, the markets, the taxes, the zoning, the politics, the weather.

Save the exotic new location for a branch once your business is thriving!

18

TIME MANAGEMENT

Women frequently play more than one role in our society. If you are one of those women who has one or more children, a spouse, or an aging parent, for instance, you will have multiple demands on your time. The way to succeed in your business is to carve out a chunk of time—probably at least eight hours a day, five or six days a week, maybe more—and make sure all of those with whom you interact or who are dependent on you understand that this portion of time is essential to your business.

Many businesswomen have found that they can manage their households and dependents more effectively because of the skills they have learned at the office. There is an old theory that the best way to get through any day is to make a list of ten things you want to get done and then do only the top thing on your list. The theory goes that if you do that every day, by the end of ten days you will have the ten most important things on your mind accomplished.

If you are working out of a home office, do not let people waste your time. Do not let them belittle your company operation. You are not "free" when you are home.

Business hours. If one of your motivations for starting your business was greater flexibility in your time commitments, make sure that you build that into your realistic plans. However, the outside world should always view you as open for business Monday through Friday 9 AM to 5 PM. If you or qualified staff cannot be on hand during those hours, make sure that you've covered yourself with an answering machine, a fax machine, a computer.

19

THE FEASIBILITY STUDY

Any new business requires a feasibility study, which determines whether your idea can exist as an ongoing profitable business. Such a study needs to provide or consider:

1. a description of your product or service
2. existing competition
3. plans for pricing your product or service
4. a list of likely customers
5. a list of likely suppliers
6. staff needs
7. space requirements, including the possibility of leasing commercial real estate
8. equipment, including the pros and cons of leasing versus purchase
9. startup money required
10. cost of startup money and likely sources
11. your background and ability to manage such a business, including previous management, sales, and new product development experience.
12. additional skills required and whether you are going to seek additional training or hire someone with these skills
13. growth potential—in other words, in addition to the market you perceive for it now, do you also perceive a market three, five, ten years down the line, and on what research do you base that perception?
14. your likely customers, and how you are going to reach them—direct mail, telemarketing, paid advertising

If your business is going to involve direct mail, it might be wise at this point to do a small direct mail test. It is usually possible to read the results of a small test and make relatively accurate projections for one to three years based on those results. Lending institutions are frequently willing to lend seed money for a small direct mail test prior to a larger commitment because they too feel results can be read and projected.

20

THE BUSINESS PLAN

Many of the elements of your feasibility study will be incorporated into your business plan. Your business plan defines what your business is going to do, states its purpose, identifies its product or services and projects both the income and expense side generally in great detail for one year and in somewhat less detail for three to five years.

The business plan also includes a description of the owner's background, where applicable, and responsibilities in the new business. Similar information is assembled for other partners or key employees.

On the expense side, the business plan identifies those expenses necessary on day one, such as insurance, equipment, stationery and office supplies, appropriate licenses and permits, as well as expenses projected for the one-year and three- to five-year periods. These latter expenses would include manufacturing, distribution, direct mail, sales commissions, retirement of bank debt, all leases.

On the income side, projections should be realistic about sales and the likely point at which income from those sales will be collected. For instance, if it takes three to six months to produce your product or service, another month to sell it and ship it, and another ninety days to collect the money and determine how much bad debt is likely, this business is looking at a money-losing scenario for at least a year and a half, and possibly two or three years. In some cases that makes sense.

A business plan will show you how much money you require on hand until income starts coming in. It is the entrepreneur's general tendency to estimate expenses low and income high and fast. Reality inevitably shows that expenses run higher than expected and less money comes in and it comes in slower than predicted. Banks know this and always adjust figures accordingly. A good lawyer and accountant assisting you in your start up will know how to make these modifications as well.

Once you've covered all the bases and are ready to start, take your expense estimate for the first year and double it. Now you're really ready to start.

Outside experts. When preparing your business plan to present to potential business partners or investors, be sure to take maximum advantage of experience you have had by presenting it in a way that shows you can handle large amounts of money, sell, supervise staff, and do long-range planning. It might be wise to bring in a professional to assist you with developing the feasibility study, business plan and any presentations to partners or investors.

21

BUSINESS ORGANIZATION

If you are satisfied with the results of your feasibility study, and determine that your idea is, indeed feasible, you are ready to launch your business either as a sole proprietorship (you're the owner, you run the business, you make all the decisions, you carry all the risk), or as a partnership (you share decisions, you share responsibility, you share the risk and you share the profits). You may wish to incorporate. There are tax advantages as well as a certain personal liability protection afforded by this.

Most women own their businesses as sole proprietors. According to the United States Census Bureau, only four percent of the female-owned businesses are partnerships and six percent are small corporations.

Should you incorporate? There is one tremendous advantage to being incorporated, and that is that you are not personally liable for the debts or mistakes of your corporation. Only the corporation's assets will be at risk if something goes seriously wrong.

On the other hand, it is expensive to incorporate, and once you are incorporated, you do face double taxation. The corporation will be taxed and then you will be taxed on the salary you draw from the corporation. There is one possible variation, however, and that is the S-corporation, which is a small closely held corporation where the losses and profits of the corporation pass directly to the owners, who are liable only to the extent of their investment in the company.

Partners. On the issue of whether you want active partners, you should consider whether your main motivation in starting this business was freedom and control. If that was the case, you should probably opt for employees rather than partners. An active partner will expect to be involved in every important decision, the direction of the company, financing, and sharing of the profits. You will have less control.

Going into business with a friend. The advantage of going into business with a friend is that you start off with someone you know, trust, and understand. The disadvantages are similar to those you encounter when you bring in family members. Although emotionally you may have a strong attachment to these people, once they're on board, if they do not perform, it can be difficult to discipline them, direct them, teach them, and worst of all, fire them.

In starting a business with a friend you have to determine who is in charge. Even in partnerships where there is a 50-50 ownership arrangement, day-to-day operating responsibility still needs to be in the hands of one person.

You would do well to go through the exercise of writing down the strengths you bring to the business and writing down separately the strengths that your friend brings to the business. You should make yet a third list of those strengths you will need to bring in from the outside.

Then try to make a practical determination about the person most suited to the day-to-day inside operation and the one most suited to represent your company to the outside world (clients, suppliers, the press).

Each of you should put in writing what it is you want from the business in the short term and in the long term. Also put in writing how you see your role and the role of your friends. Then the two of you should see how your views mesh. If they seem unbalanced, you might want to consult outside advisors.

As with spouses working together, it is highly likely that you and your friend will fall into the behavior patterns of your friendship. It will be difficult to change those patterns in a business environment. If one of you has always dominated, socially or intellectually or financially, it is likely that you will seek those same roles in a business relationship.

Any business partnership that does not work out leads to a painful situation. The pain is greatly increased when the failure is between friends.

22

NAMING YOUR COMPANY

It is essential to be direct and not "cute" when you name your company. If you are selling a service and you are the main provider of the service, as in a consulting company or a creative services company, you should put your name in the name of the company so that it is perfectly clear that the client is buying the services of the well-known person in that area—you.

If you're selling a product, you might also want to use your name as well as the name of the product. The product name should describe what it is or does. In other words, if you have a company that makes picket fences and your name is Smith, a good name for your company would be Smith Picket Fences, Inc. Cute or whimsical names that do not tell immediately what your company does can be a serious mistake. Remember that the name of your company will not be used just on your letterhead, but will appear in various industry directories, the yellow pages of the phone book, government listings, etc.

The sure way to get listed improperly is to have a name that tells nothing.

There is also the matter of institutionalizing your life's work. If you have spent your corporate and entrepreneurial life in a particular pursuit and have been fortunate enough to gain a certain fame or recognition, it might well be your desire to have your work go on, in your own name. Once you are no longer active in the business, unless your name is part of the actual title of the business, people will no longer make the association, and your business could drop off or disappear entirely.

23

LEGAL MATTERS

Try to keep your legal dealings to the necessary minimum. Make sure that all contracts and leases are well thought out and that you are not left vulnerable by them. Do not commit to what you cannot realistically deliver. If your reliable attorney is present and active at the beginning of any business relationship you establish, you should be able to head off potential disasters down the line. You do not want to run up outrageous legal fees for problems you could have prevented at the outset. You do not want to litigate. Many small businesses have disappeared under the weight of unnecessary and enormous legal expenses and lawsuits. Try always to use your lawyer to prevent problems before they happen.

Licenses and permits. If you are planning a product or service in foods, restaurants, child care, dangerous chemicals and equipment—the list goes on and on—be sure to check first about local requirements for licenses and permits. To illustrate the importance of this, I mention a charming small restaurant that opened about five years ago directly across the street from my daughter's elementary school. Everyone welcomed the restaurant to the neighborhood. It was pleasing to look at and the food was excellent. The owners were gratified at the early reception they received in the neighborhood. Then disaster struck. When they applied for their liquor license (an essential for a restaurant that serves dinner), they discovered a little-known rule that bars and restaurants with liquor licenses cannot be located within so many hundred feet of schools. The restaurant limped along for the next two years mainly on its lunch business and then relocated about six blocks away, incurring major expenses in renovation, old lease termination, new insurance, etc.

Zoning. Zoning restrictions can be a problem if you are working at home. Be sure to check in your residential area or in your commercial area should you decide to take commercial space.

Before you launch your business. Before you open your door for business, prepare a will and pick an executor. Although your business may not have made a penny yet and you may feel like you have nothing but debt to leave someone, this is not the case. It is essential that you prepare a will so that your assets go to the person or persons of your choice. In addition to your business, which may be a corporation, you have your home, personal possessions, automobile, life insurance policies. You need to think carefully about who should inherit your business. If there is no spouse in the picture, and only young children, it is important to establish a trust under the management of an experienced trusted advisor to manage or sell your business, with the proceeds earmarked for distribution to your children at the appropriate age.

In selecting an executor, keep in mind that you need someone able to handle the technical and professional end of your life as well as overseeing the future of your business and the possible participation of your heirs in it.

If it is your desire to leave all of your possessions to a spouse, and your spouse has no interest in running your business, make provision for management of it or sale of it with the assistance of professional advisors such as your lawyer, accountant, banker, and possibly insurance broker.

A trust would permit your company to pass directly to a beneficiary outside of your estate. There are numerous types of trusts, and it is wise to discuss their advantages and disadvantages with your banker, accountant, and attorney. To simply take the position that in the event of your death, your business will go to your spouse or your children is simplistic and dangerous.

24
ASSISTANCE AND INFORMATION

The federal government, as well as many state governments, sets aside a certain percentage of contracts for government work for women and minorities. (See Key 14.)

The Small Business Administration also sponsors and licenses small business investment companies that fund small business startups. Their address is 1156 Fifteenth Street NW, Washington, D.C. 20005.

The American Association of Minority Enterprise may also be helpful to you (915 Fifteenth Street, NW, Washington, D.C. 20005).

Keep in mind that the Small Business Administration devotes a lot of its time to financing the businesses of those who are disadvantaged in some way. They do, however, provide partial financing for other operations as well.

The Small Business Administration Office of Women's Business Ownership may be the best source of information for female-owned and operated businesses.

In addition, all major cities have a number of important support groups for female entrepreneurs. In New York, for instance, seminars are regularly scheduled by major banks as well as several of the universities. (Banks are anxious to have the business of female entrepreneurs.)

There are also a number of national organizations such as The Women's Forum, with branches in major cities, that provide information and assistance in a number of ways.

And last, The National Association of Women Business Owners, 655 Fifteenth Street NW, Washington, D.C. 20005 (202-293-1100) is the largest organized group of female entrepreneurs.

Take advantage of all publications and assistance you might receive through the Office of Women's Business Ownership in Washington, D.C.

25
RAISING MONEY

It is the '90s. The 1990s so far are a more difficult decade than the '80s in which to raise money for new ventures. Tax laws have changed, the climate on Wall Street has changed, and the mood of investors of all kinds, including banks, is much more conservative than it was in the 1980s. If your analyses of your new business idea, including a feasibility study and a business plan, indicate that it is a worthwhile investment for someone on the outside, you should assess the conditions under which money is available and the main sources:
1. friends and relatives
2. banks
3. venture capital operations

If the main reason you have started your business is to have control, you will not be interested in giving away anything more than forty-nine percent of your business no matter what your financing needs. If making a great deal of money is your main motivation, you will not be interested in a borrowing arrangement whereby your profits for many years go to your investors before you get your piece. I caution again, you might be better off starting small and slow than borrowing a lot of money, taking on real estate lease commitments or inventory, and giving away a large piece of your company before you know how it's going to do.

All women entrepreneurs should be aware that there are state and local funds available for contracts with women-owned and minority-owned businesses. It is certainly worth checking into the possibility of your being eligible for participation in the funds set aside for dealing with women-owned businesses.

Most women, however, use their own money or their

families' money for starting a business and do not rely on outside sources.

Outside money comes with strings attached, such as potentially high interest rates, investors with whom you have to share decisions and profits, and, in effect, a form of committee approval over your operation.

Today it is unusual for a woman not to have her own credit history and in fact not to have worked at some point, had a bank account, had credit cards. Nevertheless, for those who have no credit history, it will be essential to have a family member or friend or associate co-sign for any loans or credit lines at commercial banks. Money from venture capital sources would probably be non-existent for a woman with no business experience.

The Small Business Administration (nationally), as well as similar organizations on a statewide level, has funds earmarked especially for female entrepreneurs. Those administering these programs seek particularly worthwhile female owned startups. Information regarding qualifying for these small business loans and other forms of financing is available from the national and state offices.

After years of enduring criticism regarding their lending practices to women, commercial banks are particularly sensitive to the financing needs of female-owned and operated companies. In many of the large banks, an entire staff is assigned to encouraging and servicing this particular end of their business.

Less well known are the opportunities afforded by some of the largest and leading corporations in America. Many of these have funds available to assist in startup businesses in areas ancillary to their central business. The way it generally works is that the small business is funded by the large corporation with the corporation owning a significant chunk and having the option to own most or all of the company at a pre-determined date. Under certain circumstances, this can be a very appealing arrangement for the female entrepreneur.

26

CASH REQUIREMENTS EARLY ON

When you start up your business, or plan to start up your business, you may find it difficult to buy on credit the office supplies and office equipment which you need. Unless you have an established credit rating in your own name and some history that these suppliers can look to, they may make you pay cash for the first several months until you are established. This possibility should be anticipated in the size of the cash reserve you plan to have on hand when you start your business.

Opening up a credit line. Regardless of whether or not you need outside cash to launch your business, or even to operate it the first year, it is important to open up a credit line at your bank. The bank will assess the value of your business, your management experience, your projections, your personal credit history. Based on these criteria and others, they will establish a credit line for you. This is important in the event that you have some immediate need for cash. If you don't need to use it, don't. There's no point in owing money unnecessarily. On the other hand, if you have a need for it that makes sense and you repay it on time, it will build your credit rating and most probably lead to an expansion of your credit line.

The main advantage of an existing credit line is that when you need the money, you will not find it necessary to go through the fairly lengthy process of loan approval at the time. You may already have a loan, for say equipment or inventory, at the bank. You need a credit line anyway. You should have both ongoing relations with your bank.

Establishing a good credit rating. In addition to the bank, you will need to establish relationships with an accountant, a lawyer, suppliers, real estate brokers, car leasing companies. All of these people will be interested in your current credit rating. You have to show that you have been responsible in what you have borrowed and in the timeliness with which you have paid back your debt.

If you are planning to start your business in a year or more, it would be wise to do everything you can to improve your credit rating. First of all, it makes sense to consolidate small credit card and department store accounts into one bank loan that you pay off in installments. You will find that you probably only need one or two credit cards in your business dealings for renting cars, booking hotel and car reservations, travel, and entertaining business associates.

Second, make sure that if you carry a home mortgage, you have made your monthly payments on time.

Be certain that you are not personally overextended with debt in excess of twenty percent of your net income (less mortgage payments).

If you choose to establish your business with a partnership, your investors will most certainly want to see copies of your current credit rating report. Keep in mind that you have the right to review your file at a credit bureau at any time. It is, of course, sensible for you to see it, especially to correct any errors, before giving anyone else access to it.

27

FINANCING THE ONGOING OPERATION

You may have started your business with your own money from savings but you will most likely require additional funds to maintain or grow your new business. One source of such money is of course a bank, where you might be able to arrange a long-term or short-term *loan,* probably secured by the assets of your business.

Another method for ongoing financing is making available *equity* in your company—in other words, selling shares in the company to investors. In the case of bank debt, when you pay off a loan, you are no longer obligated to the bank. In the case of an equity investor, the investor will expect to share forever in the profits of the company. Some investors even wish to participate in the management of the company, a situation you might want to avoid. Your lawyer will structure the deal to meet your needs.

In order to raise money from investors or banks, in addition to selling your company and the long range prognosis for its product or service, you will also and most especially be selling yourself. Small businesses rise and fall on the ability of the entrepreneur. Banks (potential investors who have known you for all or most of your professional life and have a high opinion of your abilities) will be the most likely lenders.

Debt. Once you have your company moving along successfully and can show two or three years of growth and positive cash flow, you will find that banks will be extremely interested in lending you money to expand. This is very tempting indeed, especially after struggling for several years. Banks will generally lend you money based on a formula regarding your cash flow and growth percentage. Be careful. Although you may have enjoyed two or three years of continuous impressive growth, you can't be sure you will carry on like that forever. The economy could change, interest rates could change, the environment for your service or product could change, new competition could evolve, you could lose a key employee—the list goes on. When you do your one-year, three-year, and five-year projections, always do a best-case scenario and a worst-case scenario. Never borrow on the results of the best-case scenario. Only borrow on the results of the worst-case scenario. It is easy to get overleveraged. If this happens to you and one, two or three years down the line you can't service your own debt, you could lose everything—your company, your employees, your reputation. Never expand unless there is a good reason to do so. Never borrow for space, employees, promotion, or perks that are really not necessary to your business.

Losing a business you've founded and nurtured is much worse than losing a job in someone else's corporation. Many entrepreneurs don't recover completely. Entrepreneurs can find that it is very difficult to get back into the corporate world after a financial disaster.

28

WHAT TO DO IF THE MONEY RUNS OUT

Having your money run out can be quite different from having your business fail, although frequently one leads to the other. Having your money run out can come from overestimating revenues and underestimating expenses, taking on extra unplanned-for expenses, or having trouble collecting your accounts receivable. At any rate, most new businesses do not have a sufficient cushion to protect them against what could be a year or more of negative cashflow. If your business is good and the response to your product or service is good but your cash is gone, you have a number of options.

You can take your current financials and business projections to a bank and try to negotiate a loan. They may require that you use your business assets as collateral.

A second option is to seek out investors. Investors will be more difficult to deal with when your money has run out than they are when you have a great cash flow. They will certainly have their opportunity to take advantage of your dire straits. They may seek more than fifty-one percent ownership of your company, in effect removing you from the controlling role, or they may seek a large chunk of profits for several years down the line. It may be worth it.

Finding yourself in a no-cash position is difficult and frustrating and you will most certainly require the services of a lawyer, accountant, and banker, and possibly an investment advisor.

Finally, this is also the kind of time when an existing minority investor may seize the opportunity to press you for a controlling interest in exchange for just enough cash to get you buy. This is probably a bad deal.

29

PERSONAL CASH

Prepare a cash flow estimate for the next one to three years. Be conservative in your estimates. Take into consideration the effect of inflation.

Inflation is always with you. While you have certainly thought to include the effect of inflation in your business projections, make sure that you include them in the projections regarding your personal finances as well, or you may find yourself in need of drawing more money personally from the business than previously anticipated. If your profit margin is thin, this mistake in calculating your own financial requirements over a one- to five-year period could be the difference between a business that is slightly profitable and one that is losing money.

Since many start up businesses take many years to turn, that is to become profitable, you should be prepared for the possibility of several years of living below the standard of living to which you have been accustomed.

The importance of savings. Ideally, by the time you establish your own business, you will have developed the habit of saving. When you do your calculations regarding the money you will need to draw from your business, be sure to always allocate the portion for savings. The American savings rate in general is far lower than other industrialized countries with which we compete. This hurts us.

You need savings for known as well as unknown needs ahead. College tuition, retirement, caring for an aging parent, health crises, and divorce. These are just some of the situations that will require savings.

KEOGH plan. Consider establishing a KEOGH retirement plan for yourself. This plan defers taxation on self-employment income. You can contribute up to $30,000 or twenty-five percent of your earnings per year (whichever is smaller). This money is not taxed until you begin to withdraw it after you retire.

30

SAVINGS AND INFLATION

The effect of compound interest on your savings can be dramatic.

If you invest $10,000 today in a situation in which compounded monthly interest is paid, you will achieve the following effect in ten years:

At 7 percent—$20,097
At 8 percent—$22,196
At 9 percent—$24,514
At 10 percent—$27,070

To continue, after 15 years at 10 percent interest, you will have $44,539. At 20 years, also at 10 percent, you will have $73,281.

Even at 7 percent, your money will more than double after ten years. However, there is a catch. You must also take into account the effect of inflation. Remember the double-digit inflation of the late 1970s? People saw the value of their savings shrink drastically.

How inflation affects you. It is essential that you calculate the effect of inflation in your personal as well as business financial planning. Since inflation at some level has become a normal part of economic life, you must expect your costs to rise. You may also plan to increase the prices you charge for your products or services to compensate for these increased costs.

The following chart shows you how the value of your dollar shrinks over the course of ten years, at various rates of inflation.

Effect of Inflation
Rate of Inflation

Years	5%	6%	7%	8%	9%	10%
1	95¢	94¢	94¢	93¢	92¢	91¢
2	91¢	89¢	87¢	86¢	84¢	83¢
3	86¢	84¢	82¢	79¢	77¢	75¢
4	82¢	79¢	76¢	74¢	71¢	68¢
5	78¢	75¢	71¢	68¢	65¢	62¢
6	75¢	71¢	67¢	63¢	60¢	56¢
7	71¢	67¢	62¢	58¢	55¢	51¢
8	68¢	63¢	58¢	54¢	50¢	47¢
9	65¢	59¢	54¢	50¢	46¢	42¢
10	61¢	56¢	51¢	46¢	42¢	39¢

As you can see, if your money is earning compound interest at 7 percent a year and inflation is averaging 7 percent a year, you are barely holding your own. For your savings to actually increase in value, you must be earning interest at a rate that is higher than the rate of inflation.

31

CASH FLOW

The type of business you start will give you a certain cash flow pattern. For instance, if your business is swimming pool maintenance in the Northeast, you will know that your cash will not start any earlier than May and will pretty much disappear by the end of September. On the other hand, if your service is after-school day care, you may know that your cash flow will be predictable in advance since you will be asking people to pay at the beginning of the school year, it will have basically a nine-month life, and you will have a great deal of control since you will have the money up front. Then again, you may have a service business where you offer public relations services for religious institutions. While on the surface it might appear that that is a twelve-month predictable cash flow, it most probably is inactive during the summer months. Finally, if you open a restaurant, you could struggle literally for years before you do more than break even while you establish your reputation and while you await the all-important reviews from the appropriate press.

When you project your cash flow in the early stages of planning your business, do your best to anticipate seasonality and any lag time between opening your business and likely acceptance.

Collecting what's owed you. You might find it simpler, less time consuming, and in the end less expensive to farm out to an outside agency your invoicing, billing, and collection for your product or service. When you have a small business, there are those who will try to take advantage of you by paying late or even not at all on the assumption that you are in no position to do a lot of follow up. While this is generally the exception, one or two accounts like this can be an inappropriate diversion for the entrepreneur.

Since your cash flow will probably be tight in your early years, billing and collecting on time will be crucial to your operation.

On the opposite side, however, you must remember that even though you are small, you will be expected to pay your bills in a timely fashion as well. Many suppliers are hesitant to lend to a small company because of past experience with small business failures. Build a good record for yourself by not overextending yourself and by paying on time. You might wish to engage your accountant perhaps one day a month or one day every other week to handle this matter for you.

Purchasing. When you start your business and throughout its operation, always seek competitive bids from suppliers, whether leasing or purchasing. You will be amazed at the differences in prices for identical items. Don't be in a hurry. Suppliers are apt to quote the highest possible price if they know you need something quickly and have nowhere else to turn. Take your time, review your bids, and then make your decision. Also, pay all of your bills on time and where possible take discounts available for prompt payment.

What to do with the profits. If you are one of those fortunate few whose business is profitable right away or early on, you might very well be tempted to write yourself a big bonus check on the optimistic theory that your business will just keep getting more profitable. You should be cautious. Before any big bonuses, you should pay off all debt and have a contingency fund in a liquid asset equal to six to nine months of current expenses. You should also consider setting aside up to fifteen percent of your after-tax profits for research and development.

You might want to upgrade your equipment, such as the computer system you use, so that business correspondence, billing, and promotion capacities are expanded.

Personal emergency fund. You need an emergency fund. You should set aside cash equal to ninety days of your current expenses. Put this in a savings account or money market fund—something liquid.

32
TAXES, TAXES, TAXES

There are tax implications to virtually every financial decision you make regarding your business—how you finance the business, how you pay your employees, how you pay your suppliers, how you lease or buy your equipment, how you lease or buy your office space. Do not make any of these decisions without first consulting either your accountant or tax attorney.

Tax issues are extremely complicated on the federal, state, and local level, and laws keep changing. To act too quickly in this area without proper advice is literally to throw away money.

Keep good records. The IRS will be very interested in your operation, no matter how small it is. It is essential that you keep detailed and proper records of all financial transactions, no matter how small. It is easy and tempting to put off keeping your house in order because of the press of seemingly more immediate or more interesting matters. This is a big mistake. First of all, the IRS will take a very dim view of any unsubstantiated business expenses. Furthermore, you are apt to miss legitimate deductions if your record keeping is sloppy or nonexistent. An audit is an expense you don't need.

33

DISCRIMINATION

Although technically, discrimination against women in business and banking is legally over, discrimination does rear its head in subtle ways on many fronts. If you suspect that a bank or a real estate broker or landlord or a supplier is illegally refusing to do business with you, you should refer the matter to your attorney. Your attorney will know the steps to take to eliminate the problem.

On the other hand, some women feel they are the objects of discrimination when in fact there is some misunderstanding. Because women going into their own businesses are less likely to have had a long uninterrupted business career, a long uninterrupted banking relationship and credit rating, and professional, long-standing relations with a banker, an accountant, and a lawyer, it is prudent to be extremely cautious when preparing any forms or documents in application for funds, real estate, supplies. If there is any question in your mind about how to handle these, do them with your attorney. In many cases you will have the required background or knowledge or history but may be unaware of exactly how to present it.

Women in business are expected to behave like businessmen. Frequently this means going along with seemingly endless sports-oriented and locker-room-type conversations during sales pitches, at conventions, wherever people in your field gather.

When I entered the business world I was frequently the only woman traveling with the entire sales force at my first corporation. I would be in attendance for all business sessions but tended to stay by myself during the "free time." I could have tried to join in with the sports anecdotes and the dirty jokes, etc., but I chose not to.

I also chose not to put it down. I simply didn't participate. I have noticed that as more women enter various professions, they have had a major impact on subjects of conversation at corporate and company and industry gatherings. I now frequently see clusters of women gathered together to discuss childcare, divorce, remarriage, and bad attitudes perceived on the part of older men in particular.

Interestingly, there is a further evolution in this issue. Young men and women, right out of college and graduate school, seem to have a great deal in common and have a lot to say to each other. The search for common ground seems to be a generational issue.

Do male-dominated corporations and businesses wish to do business with female owned and operated businesses? In our competitive age, the answer is generally yes, if the female owned company offers the best price, the best terms, the best product, the best service, the best delivery—whatever is required. Younger businesses, such as computer software, have hired large numbers of women who have made their way to the top. This is a relatively recent development.

Providing a product or service to a younger business can be easier than dealing with some long time male dominated mature industries.

34

MULTIPLE BUSINESSES

If you are one of those entrepreneurs who start a business mainly for the thrill of taking something small and turning it into something large or taking something from start to finish, you may find yourself tired of your core business after several years. If your skills are truly entrepreneurial, you are the type of person who will spot business opportunities all the time. You may be unable to resist a fabulous opportunity and may, in fact, find yourself starting a second business and either turning your first business over to a senior trusted employee or selling it. Many famous entrepreneurs have started five or six businesses. They have figured out that their main skill is in the development and launch.

In order to operate in this fashion, the entrepreneur needs to be skilled not just in spotting business opportunities and developing them, but in the all important area of delegating. If you are the whole show, there is no way you can turn your business over to someone and expect it to thrive. If you are an entrepreneur who can delegate, congratulations.

35

LEARNING TO DELEGATE

If your experience is corporate, you will already know the importance of delegating. It makes you look good to hire and train and promote the best people you can find. Giving them autonomy and lots of opportunity is good for you. It is shortsighted to fear hiring people who could replace you. If you hire, train, and promote someone who could in fact replace you, you're ready to move on to even bigger things. Delegating is particularly important in your own business, where it is tempting to do everything yourself. Sometimes it seems easier than explaining, organizing, and even hiring. This is a serious mistake. If your skills are truly entrepreneurial, you need to be the one person with the long-range view, you need to dream. You need to take risks. You need to venture into unknown areas. This process can be time consuming, in fact practically full time. If you are the sole proprietor of your business, no one will care about your business the way you do because no one will have as much at stake. Consequently, you need, from Day One, to involve your employees at the highest possible level. Good people rise to the challenge; mediocre people should be replaced.

36

MAINTAINING A COMPANY MAILING LIST

No matter what your business, it is essential that you maintain an accurate and up-to-date mailing list of *everyone* you are dealing with and have dealt with. This should be categorized by clients and customers, suppliers, services, promotion outlets, prospects, and any other significant categories. This list will be of great importance and use to you many times. First of all, properly maintained, it will show the growth of your business, the growth and changes in those whose services you require, and the growth in your universe of prospects and promotion outlets for reaching those prospects. You will use this mailing list and/or data base for testing new products and services, thanking existing customers, and resurrecting former customers.

In many industries, such as the publishing industry, you can even rent your list to other non-related interested companies for a handsome profit. This list will also be important to potential bankers, investors, partners, and buyers.

Use this list as often as possible to stay in touch with people. Inexpensive post card reminders and announcements can be very effective.

Remember to keep a copy of your updated list off the premises, most probably in a safe deposit box along with other important documents.

37

TRAVEL AND ENTERTAINMENT

Establish a realistic travel and entertainment budget for yourself. These are expenses that you incur traveling or entertaining potential clients, suppliers, and publicity-related people. If wisely spent, this money permits you to be visible, keep in touch with your network of business associates, and provide some entertainment, such as annual Christmas and holiday parties, for employees.

Business travel. There has always been a certain glamour associated with business travel. The beautifully dressed female executive boards a plane in New York for a one day meeting in Chicago or a two day meeting in Houston, or wherever—it's made to look stressless, fun, exciting. Actually business travel is tiring, expensive, frequently boring, and almost always inconvenient. You and your new employees should travel only when necessary. With the advent of the fax machine and advanced telephone and computer hookups, it may be possible for you to avoid major travel expenses altogether.

It is also wise to monitor the alleged travel requirements of your employees and to discourage at all times those trips that are motivated more by a convenient vacation hookup than by any real business need.

Company cars. Many employees from large corporations are accustomed to having a company car. The company usually covers the cost of all business-related expenses and the employee is expected to pick up the cost of the car during personal use. In actuality, this can be a difficult distinction and lead to some misunderstanding. *Most* employees do not require a company car. Before deciding to make one available for an employee, do a comparative study of the cost of reimbursing your employee for use of his or her own car and public transportation versus the cost of leasing and insuring a company car. It can be difficult to get out of a lease if the employee leaves and you no longer want the car. Insurance is expensive. This is an important item worth checking out thoroughly.

38

THE OFFICE

Your office should look like an office, whether you're in an office building or operating out of a room in your home. If it's in your home, set it up in a professional way and make it off limits to other members of your family. If you receive clients, customers, or suppliers in your office at home, make sure that the entranceway that they use is also as professional as possible.

Office location. If you have definitely decided that you cannot run your business out of your home, you need to look for office space. If the function of your office is to handle correspondence, telephone, record keeping, and be home base for a sales force selling the product or service, you need a reasonably-priced, efficient, safe office space. It need not be luxurious. Each of your employees should have enough room to work comfortably, and you should have enough room to do day-to-day work and to hold meetings. If your employees, especially sales people, make sales calls by car, you do not need to locate yourself in a central or high-traffic area.

If, on the other hand, your employees and representatives are making calls in the immediate vicinity, it helps to be located near your customers so that your people can go out on sales calls or bring prospects conveniently and easily into your office space, perhaps to view video presentations. Security is always important, but if there are only a few employees, it becomes critical. The building should be secure, the elevators and hallways should be monitored and there should be only one access to your office space, preferably in a high visibility area. You do not want to be alone at the end of the hall or near a fire escape or in a dark area or near an unmonitored service elevator.

If your need is for *retail space,* you will have quite a different set of priorities. Your main objective will be high traffic, traffic of the sort that buys your product. Safety will be an issue. The general prosperity of your area will also be an issue. A cheerful, accessible, well-lit, safe space in a high-traffic area, safe, up-and-coming location is ideal. It is more important that your space meet those criteria than that it be huge. There are a number of inventive ways to handle small space, but virtually no way to build traffic in an out-of-the-way, undesirable, or unsafe location.

Your insurance company will be very interested in the type of space you have and the security in your area, and these aspects will probably affect your premium.

Subletting space in an ongoing company. This can be the perfect solution for a startup business that does not want to incur the cost of a receptionist, mailroom, security, and furnishings. During the last ten years, many corporations took more space than they need now. Many are anxious to sublet, simply to break even. It's frequently possible to find very attractive, small, sublettable space.

Owning office space. You might certainly want to spruce up your offices, but indulging in oriental rugs and fine paintings does not make sense. If anything, you should consider giving up being a renter and buying a small office building that you might occupy along with one other tenant, thereby covering the cost of your mortgage and maintenance. This is a move to consider only if your business is very stable, relatively predictable, and substantially profitable. This potential investment in real estate could pay off handsomely in the long term. Also, should you require more office space in the future, you could take over the entire building or sell the building and buy a second, larger one where you could have the additional space you need and still have one or two tenants—basically trading up your real estate investment. The building would be owned by your business. Before making such a move, especially in a soft real estate market, check very carefully on the condition of the building, the location, transportation, services, and taxes. It is obviously not a wise move to buy a building in an area where there is a very high vacancy rate because you will never find a profitable tenant. It is also unwise to buy in an area where no one would want to work or that is so inaccessible that suppliers and clients do not want to visit.

39

STAFF

First of all, take on as little full-time staff as possible, preferably only one other person. Use freelance help wherever you can. During the last twenty years, when unemployment has been running moderately high, there has been plenty of talent available on all levels for large corporations as well as small businesses. However, in the '90s, and even in the decade beyond, there will be a skilled labor shortage in the United States. Small businesses will have to compete with large businesses for the talent they require. Small businesses are likely to attract the same types of people who start them—namely, those looking for flexibility and unconventional office setups—but the previously limitless supply of educated women at home will pretty much vanish.

Nonetheless, your business will need what are called support services. In large corporations most employees never think about the function of the mail room, the switchboard, the personnel department, or the public relations, advertising, and promotion department. These are all services that are easy to take for granted.

Your new business will have to provide all of these functions. More often than not, a single-person-owned and operated business has one person who provides all of these functions. It can be disheartening to discover how long you spend on miscellaneous maintenance work when you thought that owning your own business would be somewhat more exciting and glamorous. You will have the exciting and glamorous part, but you also need to cover these other bases.

It is unlikely that you will be able to afford full-time help in all of these areas. As a new business startup you should look to freelancers wherever possible. These are people with expertise who do not need to be put on the payroll, who require no benefits, and who are paid by the hour for the services you require when you require them. It is important to develop a network of the kinds of freelancers you will need.

40

PERSONNEL MATTERS

Although you may not be able to afford a full-time personnel person when you launch your business, you will have to fulfill personnel obligations anyway on your own. Among the obligations or functions of the personnel department are

1. establishing proper insurance for each employee and assisting with the filing of forms and follow up when necessary
2. overseeing the administrative work involved in any kind of profit sharing or pension or 401-K which you might offer employees
3. establishing a vacation policy and monitoring attendance
4. hiring and firing under the direction of the president or appointed director. This involves dealing with employment agencies, placing ads in local newspapers, screening applicants, checking references and assisting in the evaluation of employees on a regular basis. These evaluations are customarily performed once a year, although in some cases they are required every six months.

Job descriptions. Official job descriptions should be developed for every position you fill. The employee should review the job description upon being hired and at each evaluation to see if any changes are required.

It is the responsibility of the head of the company or the head of personnel, if there is one, to determine what tasks the company must carry out on a daily, weekly, monthly, and annual basis, and to divide up these tasks into official jobs and then to develop the job descriptions for each function. Each job description should also come with a recommended salary range based on the skills required for that job.

Salaries. Your new small business should pay competitive salaries for your industry or field. On top of a competitive salary, be inventive about employee benefits that you can afford and that you are able to give, benefits that your larger corporate competitor might be unable to match—such things as more flexible hours, more flexible vacation, responsibilities and opportunities beyond the job description, and attendance at special events.

It is always possible to hire someone cheap, but it rarely works. Employees who feel that they are seriously underpaid spend most of their time either resenting being on the premises or job hunting.

On the other hand, seriously overpaying someone could build a situation where the employee simply feels contempt for you, and instead of performing beyond what's called for, this employee may tend to not work to capacity.

Employee benefits. Americans view certain employee benefits as guaranteed, although there really is no guarantee. When you are hiring for your new young company, you should be prepared to offer competitive salaries and health benefits. Beyond that, it would be to your advantage to compete with the larger corporations by offering flexibility in terms of vacation, office hours, work at home. It is very difficult for a small entrepreneurial operation to offer beautiful downtown offices, pension plans, and a corporate jet.

Many recent surveys show, however, that people would be glad to give up occasional access to a limousine or other glamorous perk in exchange for flexibility in hours. Those men and women are spending an ever-increasing amount of time caring for dependents, children, and aged parents. Your company should be able to provide much greater flexibility than an enormous bureaucratic corporation. Be sure to make a point of the advantages your company offers in the benefits area during your first interview with any potential employee.

Promotions from within. Promotion from within is

usually more effective than replacement from the outside and the personnel department or person handling the personnel function should be encouraged to deal with turnover in this fashion.

Employee training. Just as additional training might be useful for you, it may also be useful for your key employees. Consider it a wise investment if the course is well-tailored to the needs of your company.

Office decorum. Everyone benefits from a certain amount of structure, and the larger the group of employees, the more useful structure is. You need to establish work hours (most commonly 9 to 5), appropriate work attire, and appropriate office behavior (proper use of the phone, proper handling of visitors, confidentiality regarding business matters).

Dress. Dress for the occasion. If during the course of your business day you have contact with the public, it is essential that you (and your staff) be attired appropriately for the office. Although one of your main reasons for starting the business may have been to give yourself flexibility, it is important that you set the right example for your employees and that you have a certain presence when dealing with suppliers, professional advisors, customers, etc.

Office politics. Office politics is generally associated with large corporations. Actually, there can be office politics in even a small office with two or three employees. This is something to be discouraged at all times. It wastes a lot of time and on occasion intimidates the best workers.

Office politics is carried on at your expense. If you don't take part in it, you set a certain example. If your door is truly always open and any employee at any level can talk with you, that sets a certain tone.

Be careful however, not to undermine your own managers. If you give a manager authority over a staff of a half dozen or so people, it is a mistake to interfere on a regular basis and go around the manager. The manager will resent it and will find it impossible to perform or to deliver the performance of his employees. The lower level employees, in the end, will have nothing but contempt for the system.

That does not mean that you are not open and cordial to their suggestions and participation. It simply means that you support managers to whom you have delegated operating and/or bottom line responsibility.

Retirement age. Should you have a mandatory retirement age for your employees and for yourself? Definitely not. Productivity and creativity do not appear to be a function of age. On the one hand, you might admire the energy level of a very young person, but on the other hand, you might also greatly admire the expertise of an older worker.

Your objective—for your employees as well as yourself—should be to permit full-time work until such time as it is no longer productive, for the company or for the individual. At that time, a move to part-time work is a sensible next step. It means the company does not instantly lose the experience of the owner or the employee, and the owner and employee do not need to experience the unpleasant shock of going from full-time work to full-time leisure. As workers get older and desire more freedom and time for travel and family or whatever, you will find it is easy to accommodate their desire for shortened hours while keeping the productivity of your company at full force.

41

HIRING FAMILY MEMBERS

With owning your own business, the option opens up to you to hire family members. There are two sides to this story. First of all, family members will generally work harder, for longer hours, and for less money because they feel themselves to be a part of the business. Sometimes these people are salaried employees, and sometimes they are partners. Many family businesses gain a stability that others lack.

On the other hand, there can be difficulties with employing family members. It is harder to be dispassionate with them, to discipline them, to direct them, and to confront the truth when it is obvious that they don't belong in the business. Families do split apart over the experience of working in the same business.

In addition, down the road when the entrepreneur is looking at retirement, if there are several heirs apparent or family members, it becomes a nearly impossible task to pick one over another.

If the retiring entrepreneur was dynamic and charismatic, the family members taking over are often up against unrealistic expectations that they will share these personal qualities, no matter how hard they work. They are frequently not taken seriously by other employees and are assumed to have a cushy, inside track.

Family members can bring you great joy and satisfaction or great grief at your company. The positive side is of course your positive personal feelings about them, your trust for them, and your no doubt optimistic view of their qualifications.

The down side is that family members are harder to

supervise, harder to transfer, harder to pass over at promotion time, and extremely difficult to fire.

If you hire your spouse, you run the danger of slipping into the husband/wife roles to which you are accustomed. This can spell big trouble in the female-owned business.

If you hire your offspring, with the long-range hope of bringing them into some kind of a partnership and ultimately leaving them the business, you have a number of difficult decisions to make. It is better to have your offspring trained elsewhere and bring them into the company at a more senior level. Offspring brought in as trainees and then quickly promoted are generally shunned and resented by other employees. An offspring trained elsewhere who brings important skills to the company that will increase the success and profitability of the company is more likely to be welcomed and supported. This person is also more likely to be able to successfully supervise older employees.

Knowing when to give significant authority to an offspring is a matter of personal evaluation. Most entrepreneurs love their companies and want to be certain that they continue to run smoothly and successfully after they begin to withdraw somewhat from the operation. It can be extremely difficult to step aside for a child ready to take over.

It can also be extremely difficult to accept the different values, culture, and time frame of the child and to adapt to their new ideas and suggestions.

42

SUMMER OR SEASONAL INTERNS

Many universities and some specialized high schools offer students as summer interns, either at no salary or at the minimum wage. The objective for the universities is to give the students first-hand experience in the field of their major interest where they get a chance to try various phases of a business and gain some insight into its operation.

From your standpoint, this is an inexpensive or free way to get highly motivated, although usually unskilled, assistance.

It is not uncommon for interns to return year after year and to become entry-level employees upon graduation. The key thing here is the motivation of the students. A motivated worker is many times more effective than a skilled, unmotivated worker.

Interns are, however, inexperienced and will require supervision and training before they will actually be useful to you.

43

BRINGING IN MANAGEMENT TALENT

If your company is thriving and you are at the center of everything, you are probably stretched pretty thin. Entrepreneurs who are successful frequently have a combination of a big dream, high energy, charisma, and optimism. Many work incredibly hard and basically do everything.

There may come a time in your business when there are management skills required that you do not have. For instance, if your company has grown substantially and competes with mid-size to large corporations, you may need the skills of a business planner, human resource director, investment advisor, or even an engineer or other technical type. Deciding whether or not to bring in management people more skilled than you, the owner and entrepreneur, is a difficult decision to make. You might opt to keep the company the size it is and to continue to run it yourself because of the enormous satisfaction you get from that. And that's okay. On the other hand, your main goal might be to develop the biggest possible business, and if so, sooner or later you will need heavy-duty talent. If you bring in upper echelon outside people, you need very specific contracts regarding their responsibilities in order to avoid an immediate conflict. You have to be willing to delegate to them the task you hired them to do. You cannot feel threatened. If you own a company outright, you always have the option of letting them go if it doesn't work out.

If, on the other hand, you have investors, they will have a say in this matter and a palace coup is always unfortunately a possibility. Discuss the matter fully with your attorney before you do anything.

44

PERSONNEL PROBLEMS

As you hire employees for your new company, you will have to deal with both the female and male reactions to having a female boss. I find that these reactions tend to run along generational lines. Educated men and women in their twenties inter-relate very well and face employment from the perspective gained in college and graduate school where men and women are on an equal footing. Employees in their thirties and forties may bring their personal emotional baggage to the job. In the case of the women, they may secretly resent a woman in a position of authority, no matter how good she is, how fair she is. Usually over time, excellence will win out. Women who personally have trouble with their own gender identity, are naturally going to have it on the job. If it gets too bad, the long range prognosis is not good.

Men in their thirties and forties may come from traditional marriages, both the marriage of their parents and their own marriage, especially the older men. They will be accustomed to watching their fathers take control and tell their mothers what to do, and perhaps at home they have the domineering role and fall into it rather automatically at the office.

The best way to change this in the new company environment is to clear the air by firmly establishing in writing and in personal contact who's in charge and why. This needs to be reinforced with exposure to the background of the female entrepreneur and her successes at her new company.

While gender-related difficulties will always be part of the employment environment, they are diminishing rapidly as employees focus on their careers, their future prospects, global competition, and a middle management bulge in corporate America, offering far fewer opportunities than previously.

Within corporations there are, of course, behind-the-scenes jokes about female personality types at the top, including "dragon lady" and "bimbo." One of the joys of the female-owned and operated business is that the female owner is in fact the owner. It is unlikely that she would be in that position for very long unless she had competence and confidence. Usually this combination is enough to erase stereotypes.

In corporate life you may have had to constantly justify your existence in a key role and even ward off sometimes very subtle sexual harrassment. Long range, you surely found that the best policy was to let success speak for itself.

In your own firm, of course, you can deal with offenders rather more swiftly and directly.

45

SEEKING THE HELP OF PROFESSIONALS

To start your business, you need the services of a good lawyer, a good accountant, and a good banker—at least. You may also need a real estate broker, an insurance broker, and an investment advisor. The best possible way to find these people is through word of mouth. If you have several personal or business acquaintances who have had long-term good relations with and service from certain professionals, those professionals are certainly worth interviewing. Do not hire the first person you see. In each case, interview at least two or three reputable, qualified professionals. Then make your decision. Be sure that you make your decision based on their ability to meet *your* professional needs. A long time family attorney, who has done only a will for you, might not be the best choice for the legal work required in a startup of a new business.

If you are unable to find satisfactory help through your circle of personal friends and acquaintances, seek the help of the appropriate trade organizations in each case. Each organization should be able to give you the names of several persons in your area who can meet your specific needs, as described by you to them.

I do not believe it is to your advantage to use the professional services of only those people recommended by one of the professionals you use. In other words, if your banker urges you to use a certain lawyer and accountant, etc., they may not be able to function effectively as checks and balances on each other. Spend the time to find them all yourself.

Advisory board. It's always a good idea to form an outside Advisory Board. Call on someone you know personally who is a lawyer, an accountant, a marketing or sales person, and someone with some government experience. You need offer no monetary compensation. You could convene your group of advisors once or twice a year over lunch or dinner at your home and use these sessions for brainstorming and discussing unexpected developments in your business. If any of these people are prominent in your community or business area, you might want to list the board members discreetly on your letterhead.

46
INSURANCE

As this book is being written, there is great pressure on the Congress to pass major changes in those laws that regulate the insurance industry. There are cries for universal national health insurance. There is pressure to lower the cost of automobile insurance. There are protests on both sides regarding the handling of liability and damage insurance.

Whatever may happen on this front, it's wise to be certain that your basic insurance requirements are met.

INSURANCE NEEDS FOR YOU AND YOUR COMPANY

For You
Health Insurance
Life Insurance
Disability Insurance
Property Insurance
Liability Insurance

For Your Company
Property Insurance
Liability Insurance
Key Man Insurance

For Your Employees
Health Insurance
Life Insurance

Health insurance. You must have coverage that will take care of you for everything from routine and minor illnesses and injuries to catastrophic long-term illnesses. There are hundreds of variations of insurance policies and it is essential to put yourself through the tedious procedure of reading about all of the types available to you. Your goal is to be protected from being wiped out by an illness or injury and to have the majority of your costs covered for you and your dependents for routine day-to-day health matters.

First of all, assess what kind of insurance you have through your employer or the employer of your spouse. You should set out to cover those areas that are missing.

If your spouse or you lose your employment and consequently your health insurance, you should know that the COBRA law requires that the insurance company convert the policy and payments to you for up to an 18-month period while you seek other coverage. If, on the other hand, you find yourself with no insurance, the risk is simply too great. It is better to have some coverage, possibly with a relatively high deductible, than none at all.

New alternatives on this front include Health Maintenance Organizations and Preferred Provider Organizations and variations on these.

Life insurance. If you have any dependents, you should have life insurance. The amount you need depends on other aspects of your financial planning, but a good rule of thumb is two to three times your annual income. If you have several dependent children or dependent ill parents, you should increase this accordingly. There are many types of life insurance policies including term, which simply covers you, for a modest annual premium, for the amount of the death benefit. Then there are others, such as whole life, that serve as savings accounts or investments for you. These pay moderate interest, the premiums are higher, and they can be borrowed against at low interest.

Disability insurance. Disability insurance is perhaps the most important overlooked kind of insurance. Your chances of becoming disabled before you are 65 are much greater than your chances of dying. Disability insurance comes in several formats, including disability payments to you if you are totally disabled or partially disabled or disabled enough so that you cannot perform your current professional job. Premiums vary accordingly. Some sort of basic disability insurance is highly recommended, since something as common as an automobile accident could, in six months time, wipe out your life savings.

Property insurance. Your possessions, including your home, should be fully insured against damage, theft, and fire. Such insurance is available at a relatively low premium when it pays only a partial reimbursement for lost property. Most expensive, but better, is replacement value insurance where the insurance company pays the replacement cost of the goods lost. It is wise to make a video tape of your dwelling and all of your possessions, with an audio track in which you partially describe the items and their value. Such tapes should be put in your safe deposit box in the event you need to file an insurance claim. It is also wise to keep a permanent record of the serial numbers of any kind of machines or appliances as well as sales receipts of all important items.

You may wish to also take out a fine arts coverage for important artwork or silver. Separate policies are also available for jewelry, furs, and boats. Automobile insurance is essential and you should discuss with your broker the proper amount for the type and age of the vehicle you drive.

Personal liability insurance. Personal liability insurance is important in the event someone has a mishap or accident on your property or using your property.

Key man insurance. This is life insurance payable not to one of your beneficiaries but to your company in the event of your death. In many cases the entrepreneur is the main asset of the business, especially in the early years. If the entrepreneur dies, the business can crumble rather quickly. Investors want some protection against this and generally demand key man insurance equal to one or two times their investment in the company.

Comparison shopping. Before you buy any kind of insurance, you should meet with an insurance broker you know and trust or one recommended by someone you know and trust. Review all of the kinds of policies available for your needs and inquire about the health of the company sponsoring these policies. There are several directories that rate insurance companies in terms of their financial health and ability to make good on claims. It's worth checking this as well. Insurance is an important investment and should be treated as such.

Never sign up for any kind of insurance policy that someone attempts to sell you in a cold phone call. In all such inquiries, always ask for something in writing.

47

PROJECTING A POSITIVE IMAGE

No matter how you feel, no matter how your business is going, it is important that you *never* complain about the status of things to either your suppliers or your clients. They need to know that you are completely in charge, optimistic, and successful. No one likes dealing with someone who feels that he or she won't succeed.

When you have a small business, it's tempting to unburden yourself of your frustrations and worries and even panic with whoever calls on the phone. This is always a mistake.

On the other hand, it is possible to be totally frank with your banker, your lawyer, and your accountant. They'll need to know the best case scenario and the worst case scenario at all times so that they can help you prepare for the cycles that any business experiences.

Publishing and speaking in your field. Because you will always be interested in broadening your customer and client base, you should seize all opportunities to speak publicly about your company and product or service or to write about these matters. The best way to build sales in any size business is through word of mouth.

Don't be intimidated by the experience of speaking or writing about something you know well. The only way to get started is to get started. Every time you speak, you will get better. Every time you write, you will gain additional expertise. Don't be afraid to take the first step in either area.

Networking. Men have always been involved in networking and it's important for female business owners to become involved as well. Networking is simply associating with and making yourself known to other people in your field or profession. It is especially helpful to associate with influential people and established people you can call on to help with the special needs of your business.

48

MARKETING

Take a hint from large corporations on how they handle marketing. They use paid advertising only when necessary. Big corporations all prefer publicity and promotion, which happen to be free. Make yourself visible. Court the local press, radio station, tv station (where available). Join your local trade organization as well as women's business groups. Make sure you do frequent press releases regarding your service or product. Welcome visits to your business location from local press, radio, etc. Give away samples of your product or service for local charitable events.

Awards. Whatever your field, there are surely trade organizations that exist to promote the field and those in it. These types of organizations generally give annual awards or recognition of some sort. Be sure to enter your product or service in any suitable competition. Do this every year, even if you did not win anything the year before. Many people prefer to do business with prestigious organizations which have won important awards.

Marketing and your competitors. Study the products and services and especially the marketing of your competitors *before* you take any serious steps toward launching your business. Be open-minded enough to learn from their good points as well as their bad points. If you face a competitor who has been in business profitably for a long time and has a good reputation, you had better be prepared to deliver a product or service with a distinctive, recognizable, explainable difference. Do not imagine that you can produce an identical product or service faster, for less, or better. Your idea and inspiration has to, in fact, be different.

If, on the other hand, a competitor is barely getting

by in an area that you believe has significant growth potential, and you can produce a similar product or service using improved methods of production, distribution and selling, your venture has merit.

When there is a direct competitor involved, the focus becomes marketing. Marketing is identifying the need for the product or service and filling it with a quality item at a reasonable, justifiable price. Marketing means knowing the potential customer and having the ability to reach that customer and sell that customer. Marketing can mean persuading the customer to switch from Brand A to Brand B. Marketing is about market share. If, for instance, there are 10,000 customers for your product and 7,000 buy your product and 3,000 buy your competitor's, you have the dominating market share. If it's the other way around, your marketing efforts need to lead to a reversal of those numbers.

Sometimes your marketing effort must actually make a market for your product or service where none has existed before. Your marketing has to build demand for something your customers didn't know they needed. This is, of course, particularly true when a totally new product or service, never before seen, is introduced. While this might look easier, it is in fact harder.

People who've been getting along just fine without your "whatever" take a great deal of persuading to change their consuming habits.

Choosing a creative services agency. If your product or service requires paid advertising or promotion beyond your ability to produce, you will need the services of an outside agency. Choosing this agency will be difficult. As a small company, you will probably want the services of another small company. Some of the big agencies do fabulous work, constantly winning awards for very visible household name products. However, these accounts sometimes generate millions of dollars for the agencies in commissions. If you are a very small account that runs only a couple of ads a year and produces only a couple of pieces of promotion and perhaps stages one publicity event, the commissions to be generated on your account will be so small that the larger agencies either will not consider you or will assign you to a beginner. You will probably be better off working with a small entrepreneurial company, like your own, where you may get the attention of the key person. A small agency trying to build business will put forth a special effort and extra time and talent.

In your advertising and promotion, be sure you are selling what you're selling. Those fabulous but ambiguous ads, where we remember the ad but not the product, are clearly not for you. If you have a small budget, you absolutely must sell your actual product or service and reach your most logical, easily accessed customer.

Whether you are doing your advertising and promotion yourself or using the services of a small agency, remember to keep it simple, direct, and be sure to sell the benefit. Do not try to get more than one message into one ad or promotion piece.

If you are doing direct mail to generate prospects for your product or service, do a small test before rolling out any large numbers of mailing pieces. Direct mail is very, very expensive, and it is essential that you read the results of your first small test and do practical, conservative estimates before proceeding with the campaign. If possible, during your test, experiment with more than one piece and possibly more than one headline approach.

Should your advertising identify a competitor? There are two theories in advertising against the competition. One favors identifying the competition and attacking head on. The other says ignore the competition and simply expound on the benefits of your product or service.

Identifying and attacking the competition might work where you have equal market share and equal name recognition, but it does not work for you if you are the new entry in the field. You run the risk of being totally forgotten in your own advertisement while reinforcing an existing product or service and its brand name.

On the other hand, in those exceptional cases when it works, risky as it is, such as Avis' "We try harder," the results can be profound.

It is safer to sell on the benefits of your own product or service and brand name because then there can be no confusion, and you might begin to develop a distinctive product presence.

49

PROBLEMS

As I mentioned at the start of the book, the main thing that differentiates female entrepreneurs from male entrepreneurs is that female entrepreneurs play many roles. Frequently they are also mother, wife, caretaker for aging parents. In fact it is the multiplicity of roles that frequently leads women into their own businesses, not to shorten their hours, but to control them.

The cost of help. The female entrepreneur with all of those other roles has to accurately project the cost of housekeeping assistance, child care, and possibly dependent parent care. Here, as in everything else, you get what you pay for. As this book is being written in New York, a full-time experienced housekeeper (five days a week, 8 AM to 6 PM) runs about $2,000 a month.

Professional child care, such as a nanny, runs about $2,500 a month. Private schools average $12,000 a year. Private nurses to care for aging or disabled parents are in the same price range as the nannies, or $2,500 a month for the top of the line.

As you can see, this quickly adds up to a large chunk of money, quite possibly twice what your company might make in its first year, assuming your company shows a profit at all.

Female entrepreneurs are, however, very inventive in solving the requirements of these other roles. One common solution is to sponsor a young high school girl from the country of your choice, where you pay her transportation to the United States and provide room and board, usually for a minimum of two years and a maximum of five years, until she ges her green card.

If it turns out that she and your family are terrifically well suited to each other, this gives you a presence 24 hours a day at home and provides a certain amount of housekeeping and child care. These arrangements are rarely perfect, however. Your au pair may become homesick and leave within a few months; she may find a way to get a green card much quicker, like marrying an American; or she may be lured away by another household.

Other options include moving local college students into your home with an exchange of room and board for minimal child care and housekeeping.

Other women move in relatives, such as healthy parents, to help manage the household. Unfortunately this can lead to more problems than it solves.

Daycare centers exist for relatively modest amounts, but there are large questions about the quality of these centers and the long-range effect they have on children.

Some female entrepreneurs are married to men who are willing to assume a fair share of child care and housekeeping duties. This tends to be the exception.

It is, therefore, not surprising that female entrepreneurs tend to start their businesses once their children are raised or especially after divorce or the retirement of their spouse.

Caring for aging parents is such a complicated issue that we cannot do it justice here. The needs of a non-disabled older person are minimal. The needs of a disabled or ill aging parent are tremendous and expensive and emotionally draining.

Divorce. If you are currently contemplating a divorce, it most certainly makes sense to complete your divorce before launching your own business. State laws are complicated, but spouses increasingly claim substantial parts of entrepreneurial businesses. It could be important not to take any official written steps towards establishing your own business before you have consulted with a matrimonial attorney who prepares the paperwork to protect you from any future claims against your business.

Creditors and investors would naturally take a dim view of matrimonial litigation interfering with your ability to manage your business.

Remarriage. If you are contemplating a new marriage, it would be wise to consider including wording covering the future of your business in a prenuptial agreement. If such a document is drawn, both your matrimonial and business lawyers should review it for you.

Loneliness. Entrepreneurs are notoriously lonely. This can be debilitating. Many entrepreneurs spend large parts of every day, or even large parts of every week with little or no human contact. One way around this is to go out of your way to establish a network of other entrepreneurs (not necessarily in related businesses). You might find it helpful to get together once a week or once a month with this group. Entrepreneurs feel particularly lonely in their hard work, in their deep worries over their finances, and even in the joy of their major successes and sales. Such a support group can be the perfect outlet for discussing all of these matters which the entrepreneurs certainly have in common.

50

PAYING BACK YOUR COMMUNITY

If your business is now established and thriving, you probably realize that one of the major reasons for your success has been the support of the people and businesses in your community. Perhaps it's time to give something back. Whatever your service or product, you might wish to begin extending a discount to senior citizens or handicapped citizens. You might want to establish a scholarship at the local high school or college for a particularly worthy student interested in your field. If you own a publication, you might wish to run free service advertisements for local charities. You could consider starting a training program for people displaced in mergers, downsizing, or closings.

51

THE ROLE OF THE OWNER

The owner of a new small business may seem to play many roles and have limitless responsibility. However, it is essential that the owner recognize the real priorities for this position.

First, the owner is solely responsible for long-range planning. Although the entire process of getting your business up and running was surely daunting, the hard part is ahead.

As the owner of a new small business, you must review the projections on which the business was launched, modify them to reflect reality, watch the cash flow *daily,* and revise your three- and five-year projections. In a small business, the owner is frequently the only person with her eye on the long range.

The owner is also ultimately responsible for the day-to-day operations of the business. This means staffing, supervising, new product development, marketing, and handling all dealings with outside experts such as lawyers, accountants, bankers, financial planners, and investment managers.

A somewhat less obvious but equally important obligation of the owner is to sell. The owner must sell herself, her company, her product or service, her marketing strategy, her growth potential. She must sell to outside experts, potential investors, clients and customers, suppliers, and, of course, employees.

The owner must be vigilant about changes in her field, her competition, her local economy.

In short, the owner must be out front, both inside and outside.

Set goals. Remember that it is your primary responsibility as the head of your business to combine the short-term and the long-term view. It is encouraging to set short-term goals and achieve them. You should set both kinds of goals. Short-term goals can be goals that require a week or a month to accomplish. Your long-term goals might require one, three, or five years. Once you've set your long-term goals, don't abandon them. Have at least a monthly review of all ongoing operations and long-term goals. In some cases it is appropriate to have weekly reviews.

52

SELLING YOUR COMPANY

Let's say you have started and run and grown your wonderful company and it has been emotionally and financially very satisfying. But you have no heir you want to bring in to the company, nor any key employee you'd like to pass the business on to. You've decided that you'd like to cash in this major asset and retire or pursue other interests with the money. You've decided to sell.

You might already have had a number of offers for your profitable company. Even if you've turned them all down in the past, you can reopen these discussions. You could opt to handle the sale yourself, but a better course is to bring in a broker or a team including your banker, accountant, and lawyer.

A five-year projection for your operation needs to be prepared. Then a general prose section needs to be developed for a formal offering document. It is very difficult to establish an asking price. Two or three years ago, for instance, media properties were changing hands at ten times earnings or more. In the current market, those same properties are changing hands at five or six times earnings. Next year will probably bring yet another scenario.

You and your team of advisors should review available information regarding prices of similar operations, and you should be realistic about the kind of price you are apt to get.

Your best prospect for your business might very well be a major competitor. Other good prospects include companies who have been anxious to branch into your area and would rather avoid a startup and instead would be interested in buying an ongoing business.

Once you have your offering document and several interested prospects, you need to turn to the issue of the terms of the deal. One possibility is a flat cash payment, and you then walk away from it. Another scenario involves a down payment, your ongoing involvement as an executive or consultant for several years, and a piece of the bottom line from your operation under the new owner for several years.

If you are willing to take a long payout, you will probably get a higher price, but it might be meaningless if the economic situation changes and the deal does not pay out the way it's supposed to. A better alternative is probably a slightly lower price and more cash on signing.

You will surely be asked to sign a non-compete agreement stipulating that you will not compete with your old company for a number of years. These agreements are strictly enforced. There will not be a possibility of your starting up a company that provides an identical service or product, based on knowledge you gained while running your former company. You will also probably be forbidden from employment by a competitor to your business.

53

SOME CASE HISTORIES

In this last section I want to pass along to you case histories of people I know—these are women who have made a major mark in their fields. In each instance I'll touch on some common obstacle which they overcame.

Public Relations. A woman at the top of the public relations world told me that when she started out, she knew that the hub of that industry was in New York but that it could be a long haul to make it all the way to the top in New York. Cleverly, she located in a large midwestern city around which were located a large number of blue chip industrial firms. Through hard work and clever campaigns, she took on at least a half dozen of them as clients. Once she had this absolutely top-of-the-line list of clients, she moved to New York where she used this list to get in the door at major New York firms. She met with rapid success in a way that she feels would have been impossible if she had simply started at the bottom in New York.

Psychiatry. The second woman, a female psychiatrist friend of mine, was associated for a long time with a prestigious hospital. She could not seem to build her private practice in the way she had hoped to. Frustrated, she got the idea that many people who could benefit from the time with psychiatrists and psychologists were logistically unable to schedule appointments because of their work day. She became one of the first psychiatrists willing to make calls at business peoples' offices. Within two years of starting this practice, her business had grown enormously, as had her name and prestige. Many others have followed her path.

Advertising. Although advertising sales forces at

major magazines are now roughly fifty percent female, not long ago it was almost impossible for a woman to get a job selling advertising for a major publication. I know several women who decided to overcome this problem by pressing hard for assignments "in the field." They showed a willingness to sell in obscure, out of the way, unpromotable areas where few advertisers existed. They showed such stellar success in these impossible-to-sell areas, that the main office was forced to promote them based on their record. As I pointed out elsewhere in this book, when you work in sales, movement can be very fast because ultimately it is based on the bottom line: How much did you sell? For these women, from this success, it was a logical step for at least one of them to start her own "rep" firm.

A woman in Los Angeles had spent the last twenty years involved mainly with her family and charitable activities. Prior to raising her children, she had spent a couple of years at an advertising agency.

The more charity work she did, the more she realized that while people are generally favorably inclined toward charities, they rarely understand what the charities do or where their contribution would go if they made one. When her children were raised, she opened a small advertising agency in Los Angeles to deal with charities and non-profit organizations. She brought a very special expertise to this work, having seen both sides of it. She kept the fees minimal, knowing how tight charitable organization budgets are. Nevertheless, she expanded rather quickly and became quite profitable early on.

Services: A woman in New York who had a mid-level management position at a bank as well as responsibility for two children, her own home, and all the etceteras, concluded that the reason she never had any free time when she scheduled days to be at home to take care of household things was that she spent the entire day waiting and waiting and waiting—for deliveries, for installation people, for repair people. She decided that she was not alone. First on the side, and then full time after quitting her job at the bank, she established a business to relieve women of the logistics of getting things done at home while trying to hold down a job at the office. She hired a lot of part-time people, at not much more than the minimum wage, to sit in people's apartments and wait. Her business took off immediately. The press picked up on what a "cute" idea it was, and now in fact she has several competitors.

A woman living near Minneapolis was caught in the sandwich generation dilemma: raising her children while caring for two aging parents. She reached the point where her stress level was out of hand, she was always exhausted, and no one was happy. She decided that the kind of day care center that she used for her children would be appropriate for her very elderly parents. First, she established her own day care business for elderly people who were simply unoccupied, not ill. She provided activities for about ten elderly people a day in her home, charging day care center rates. As her success grew and she had more applications than she could handle, she associated with a company providing day care for children and managed to work out arrangements for real estate and food services with them. This was an idea that has now caught on nationally and in fact there are some corporations now providing a combination of day and elder care on company premises.

I could go on and on with stories about women who started catering businesses in their homes and went on to managing and owning their own restaurants, women who started real estate firms staffed only with other women working short, convenient shifts bcecause of their other responsibilities, all-female law firms specializing in female businesses, the first all-female construction company.

The opportunities are there.

APPENDICES

1
SAMPLE FEASIBILITY STUDY—SENIOR DAY CARE CENTER

1. Service

The service will be a day care center for "well" seniors. This service will offer recreational, educational and physical activities for "well" seniors, Monday through Friday, 8:30 AM to 5:30 PM.

This service will also offer shorter time spans, such as fewer days a week, or half-day periods, so that those in need can customize the service to suit their schedules.

2. Existing Competition

None

3. Pricing

The service will be priced at $250 a week, full time, or by the hour for shorter stays. This pricing has been chosen because it represents about one half the cost of full-time, one-on-one care for a well senior.

4. Likely Clients and Customers

You have determined that your area is largely middle class, single family dwellings, where more than 50 percent of the families have a working husband and wife. Large numbers of seniors have come to live in the spacious homes of their children, either because of loss of a spouse, loneliness, frailty, or lack of resources to afford services in their own home and communities.

5. Supplies

This is a relatively minor aspect of this business since the bulk of the day will be spent with arts, crafts, music, and walking.

6. Staff Needs

You have checked local requirements regarding permits, and you find that you are able to operate a day care center from your home, but you must use licensed caregivers. You are planning to hire a senior athletic instructor, a part-time music teacher, and a former children's day care center teacher.

7. Space Requirement

Years ago you converted your basement into three comfortable recreational rooms, which will provide adequate space and meet local zoning and permit restrictions for ten adults, the maximum for whom you intend to provide care at any one time.

8. Equipment

You already own tables, a piano, a tape deck, comfortable chairs, and adequate dishes, silver, etc., for lunch, the one meal you intend to provide. You will have monthly expenses for materials used in arts and crafts and perhaps for updating your library of senior exercise videos.

9. Startup Money Required

You have estimated that your startup money should include three months' salary for your part time teachers, a three-month supply of arts and crafts materials, and a quarterly payment on a new insurance policy, as well as minor expenses for letterhead and phone. You have estimated the costs of a hot lunch and morning and afternoon snacks for three months.

10. Previous Experience Applicable to Such a Venture

You have raised four children, are currently caring for

one of your aging parents, and have been a part-time and substitute teacher for ten years in your local school system.

11. Additional Skills You May Need

Depending on local and state certification and permit requirements, you may need to set aside the money for evening courses for one year to gain proper certification for the program you wish to offer.

12. Growth Potential

Your growth potential should be enormous, since the population is aging at the same time that both husband and wife are in the workplace, sometimes longer than they ever expected to be, and occasionally have the additional burden of college-age children returning to live at home as well. There is a real need for your service. No one else is offering it in your area.

13. Likely Customers

Your likely customers are the aging but well parents who have returned to live with their children in your community and county. You have already interviewed dozens of them and find that the service you offer, which is largely recreational and not medical and therefore carries no stigma, would be most welcome by the seniors as well as their children.

2
ASSESSING THE FEASIBILITY STUDY

1. You have a very good fix on exactly what your service is going to offer. You've thought out how you'll do it, where you'll do it, when you'll do it, and for whom you'll do it.
2. At this time there is little or no competition.
3. You've priced your service reasonably in that you are providing group activities at half the price of one-on-one activities, and you are providing at the same time companionship, pleasant surroundings, and a home atmosphere.
4. You know who your customers are and you have already interviewed dozens of them.
5. You've considered the question of supplies and suppliers, but this is a minor factor in your business.
6. Staff requirements have been given an in-depth analysis, and you have checked on license and permit requirements. You are providing a variety of staff skills, and you are using experienced staff.
7. Your current space requirements for your startup business are taken care of in your own home. You will have no need for commercial real estate or leasing of any space off of your property. You have checked to see that you are zoned to permit a day care center.
8. Either you have equipment on hand or it is readily available and inexpensive.
9. You have available through your own funds the startup money required to cover three months' worth of expenses. You have opened a credit line at your bank to cover another six months' worth of expenses. There is no money available at this time for growth

or expansion, but that is not your priority now. You expect to watch and monitor your business for one year to see whether or not expansion is desirable.

10-12. Your teaching and family background qualify you as a caregiver. The administrative and financial skills necessary to run your business you will have to acquire in the evening courses you are preparing to take.

13. Since your original plan is to care for only ten seniors at any one time, there is definitely room for growth. This needs to be carefully assessed in terms of likely clients, seasonality of the business (the seniors are likely to take vacations when the families do), and the possibility of competition.

14. You know exactly who your customers are, and you have already reached many of them. On your small scale, personal inquiries are the best way to go. You must, if you decide to expand, budget for other means for reaching potential clients.

Because this is a simple business to start, you can do it with your own funds in your own home, and you know who your potential clients are and have already reached many of them, this business looks like a "go." You will have to closely monitor your finances, your flow of clients, the space you have allotted for each client, and any competition that might spring up. At the same time, you must watch any developments in special zoning or permits for your type of business.

As the President/Owner, you are responsible for long-range planning. Since this is a business with an immediate positive cash flow, after one year in operation, you may wish to expand.

3
THE BUSINESS PLAN—SENIOR DAY CARE CENTER

Purpose
The purpose of this business plan is to describe the senior day care center. The purpose of the day care center is to care for well seniors who live in the immediate area and who are primarily living with their grown children who are in the workplace. The day care center will provide recreation, companionship, a hot lunch and morning and afternoon snacks, some mild exercise, and arts, crafts, and music instruction.

The senior day care center will be open to all seniors who require no medical attention during their stay. The seniors can opt for a full schedule of five days a week, Monday through Friday, nine to five, or half days, or fewer days.

The center expects to provide a stimulating, warm, homelike, safe, companionable atmosphere.

Staff and Facilities
The center will be staffed by the owner (a former teacher), as well as a part-time arts and crafts instructor, a part-time music instructor, and a part-time senior athletic instructor.

The center will be housed in attractive and comfortable surroundings provided in the home of the owner. The maximum number of seniors during any given time at the center will be ten.

Finances
Appropriate licenses, permits, and insurance have been obtained. The center has incorporated and has in the bank sufficient funds to cover three months' worth of

costs and a credit line equal to six months' worth of costs.

The center expects to have an immediate positive cash flow.

Clientele *(customers)*

The owner has personally interviewed several dozen families with whom a senior (well, aging parent) is residing. These families seek a full- or part-time day care center for these seniors. The owner has also met with local political representatives of both parties, local school and church groups, and the local senior citizen chapter.

NOTE: When anticipating and planning for growth, if your idea is as successful as you hope, you should consider expanding to space in a church. Churches always need additional funds for their day-to-day operation and for charitable activities, and one of the few businesses they are able to accommodate, given their structure and place in the community, has long been day care centers/nursery schools. A day care center for seniors would seem to be equally acceptable. The space is generally attractive, safe, warm, and comfortable.

Expenses

Insurance	$ 2,500
Equipment	500
Stationery and Office Supplies	300
Licenses and Permits	250
Utilities	600
Food	4800
Staff	15,000
Salary or Draw for Owner	open
Telephone (including fax)	350
Computer	200
Postage and Mailings	200
	$24,700

Revenues
$250 per client times 50 weeks of operation times maximum ten clients = $125,000

In this relatively simple business plan, your projected revenue less projected expenses produces $100,300. If your business moves along and you have a long waiting list, you should by all means expand. If your business is an absolute smash, you should consider franchising the concept locally, then statewide and even nationally.

4
JOB DESCRIPTIONS

OWNER/PRESIDENT
Qualifications and Experience Required
- College degree
- Advanced work toward MBA, law degree, CPA all highly desirable.
- In depth knowledge of product or service offered.
- Experience in new product development, sales, marketing, budget management, bottom line responsibility, and staff management.

Responsibility on the Job
- Primary responsibility is for long-range planning, management and direction of staff, development and improvement of service or product, final approval on all financial matters including purchasing, leases, debt, and stock offerings.
- Responsible for representing the company in all matters with the industry, the press, and in community affairs.
- Primary responsibility for soliciting new business/customers/clients.
- Final approval of all staff hiring, salaries, job descriptions.
- Preparation of annual budget (with assistance of staff) and responsibility for final determination of all expenses, staff allocations, and final profit projections.

OFFICE MANAGER/ASSISTANT/SECRETARY
Qualifications and Experience Required
- College degree preferred
- One to three years' experience in field preferred.
- Background in supervision of secretarial and clerical staff and purchasing of supplies.

Responsibility on the Job
- Supervises, with approval of president, all personnel matters. Handles day-to-day contact with mid-level suppliers.
- Sets tone of the office and sets example for other staff in decorum, dress, reception to visitors, customers, suppliers, and clients.
- Orchestrates schedule for president.
- Handles required typing, dictation, filing, office management.
- Handles routine correspondence on own, for review by president.

SALES MANAGER

Qualifications and Experience Required
- College degree preferred.
- Three years' sales experience preferred.
- In-depth knowledge of industry and particular product or service.
- Previous bottom line responsibility for setting and meeting seasonal and annual sales goals.

Responsibility on the Job
- Prepare monthly and annual sales projections for service or product.
- Prepare expense budget for meeting sales projections, including staff, outside advertising and promotion, commissions, travel and entertainment, office expense.
- Develop client list and set priorities for self and or staff.
- Review existing competition and any competition expected to become active within the next one to three years.
- Set goals for advertising and promotion and set commensurate budgets.
- Supervise outside advertising and promotion services.
- Develop new product pitches, as well as ongoing updates of existing products and services.

ADDITIONAL STAFFING

Most small new businesses are launched with only the above described full-time staff. In fact, of course, many are launched by the owner who does everything.

Once the above three positions are filled, you need to

consider other services that you will require. I recommend, in all cases, that you hire these people on a part-time or hourly basis as the need arises. First of all, your new business cannot handle a lot of unnecessary overhead. Also, until you have been involved with your business for a year or longer, you won't really know what your full-time staff needs are.

The following services can be handled part time:

The Chief Financial Officer/Accountant/Financial Planner Unless your background is finance, and even if it is, you will need the help of a first-rate accountant. This person, most probably someone with an advanced degree and certification, will help you initially in assessing the financial needs of your company, the likely financial rewards, and the tax ramifications. This person will set up your books. You may call on this person to handle your monthly or bi-monthly payroll and payment of on-going expenses. This person will plot your tax strategy at least one to two years in advance.

This person should review all arrangements with suppliers and manufacturers, all real estate leases, all equipment leases. You will rely on your chief financial officer/accountant to set up your company benefits programs, such as health insurance, pension plans, profit sharing, and 401-(k) employee plans.

In very small organizations, this person also frequently functions as the human resources director/personnel director and reviews job descriptions, employee contracts, and the financial ramifications of dismissals.

Attorney/Corporate Legal Advisor. Very few companies, large or small, maintain an in-house lawyer or legal department. For purposes of this book, let's assume you will not do that at the start or further down the line.

A lawyer naturally has an advanced degree and law board certification to practice in your state. It will also be helpful if your attorney has experience in your field, experience with small business startups, and is reasonable and flexible in terms of his or her fees during your early years.

It's always tempting to seek legal assistance from a long-time friend or personal attorney who may have handled wills, estates, even a divorce in the past. Although you may know and trust such a person and be accustomed to relying on him or her for legal advice, a business startup is a very different kind of situation.

Your company attorney should be there at the very start to help you review the feasability of your business idea. The attorney can advise you on the options you have in structuring a new business, and in the options you have in financing a new business, including using your own money, that of family and friends, a loan from a bank, a credit line at a bank, or outside investors.

Your attorney should be involved in your early relations with real estate brokers and equipment leasers and in any and all contracts that you sign in the formation of your business. Your lawyer will want to work with your accountant in choosing the best accounting system for your books and the best structure for your tax policy.

Your lawyer should be able to help you avoid problems as well as be there to help you in a crisis or lawsuit. If your attorney is there to review all legal obligations in which you involve yourself, you will save yourself a great deal of money later on by heading off problems early on that could lead to legal difficulties and expensive law suits, even the loss of licenses and permits down the line.

A lawyer with experience in small business startups should be able to advise you on your sales and expense projections as well.

Sales Staff. If you have a capable sales manager in place, you can run your sales operation almost entirely freelance. Early on, it certainly makes sense to use only commissioned sales representatives, spread around the area locally, statewide or even nationwide, depending on the needs of your service or product. Your sales manager will work out benefits, salaries, and commissions based on the short-term meeting of goals. Until you are absolutely certain that your business is solid, meeting projections, not exceeding costs, and not running into unexpected difficulties with the economy or competition, it is absolutely best to keep your sales support staff freelance rather than full-time staff.

These people working on a commission basis for you may prefer to work in this manner and have several other clients. On the other hand, you may find some people willing to take commission positions with the hope that if they deliver what you need in terms of sales over a given period of time, most usually one or two years, you will bring them inside and make them full-time staff members.

Any establishment of branch offices to handle sales at this point is foolhardy.

Creative Services Director. You may have a wonderful idea for a product or service and the technical ability to produce and deliver it. However, you need to let your potential audience and buyers know about the availability of your business.

This is generally called establishing a market for your service/product. It has to be handled by professionals. It involves analyzing your service/product, positioning it, determining the strength and reach of any competition, establishing market share projections, and finally developing the creative approach to present your service/product to your buyers.

This might involve paid advertising, sales promotion such as point-of-purchase displays, and publicity support including establishing your product, your company, and you, as well as orchestrating special events to support and enhance the launch and sale of your service or product.

Full-time established advertising and promotion agencies provide these services. While all of them would like a one-, two- or three-year contract with you, including a monthly retainer, they also know that startup businesses rarely can afford to commit that kind of cash. You can find an agency that will work with you on a "by project" basis. They generally will charge you by the hour to position your product and assess your competition. They will then charge you flat fees as well as out of pocket expenses for preparation of advertising and sales promotion. These combined expenses will come to much, much less than you ever would have paid on a retainer basis. You will get what you need for your first year or two of operation at minimal cost.

Why are these agencies willing to work on this basis? For only one reason. They are gambling on your ability to pull it off, your ability to establish your company and service/product. They will then expect you to establish a more full-time long-range relationship with them because they were there, at a modest expense, when you needed them.

Secretarial/Word Processing/Typing/Filing. Your clerical, secretarial and computer word processing needs are likely to be seasonal. Make it the responsibility of your own secretary/office manager to cover these needs with freelance people. He or she should interview these people, hire them, pay them, keep track of them for later work, assess their performance, and think long range in terms of hiring one or two of them full time once you are established.

5
PREPARING YOUR PERSONAL NET WORTH STATEMENT

Your net worth is simply the difference between your total assets, what you have, and your total liabilities, what you owe. Potential lenders, investors, and partners will all want to review your net worth statement before they decide to proceed in any business arrangement with you. The categories in the chart on the following page provide guidelines for preparing your statement. Your own list of assets and liabilities may, of course, be quite different.

Net Worth Statement

Tangible Assets	Value
Residential real estate	————
Furnishings	————
Jewelry	————
Furs	————
Automobiles	————
Boat	————
Art	————
Other collectibles	————
Silver	————

Liquid or Cash Assets	
Cash on hand in savings	————
Money market funds	————
Certificates of deposit	————
Cash value of life insurance	————
Annuities	————
Any employee pension or benefit plan	————
Stocks	————
Bonds	————
Mutual funds	————
IRAs	————
KEOGHS	————
Trust Funds	————
Business Partnerships	————
Total assets	————

Liabilities	Value
Mortgage	————
Loans	————
Installment account balances	————
Taxes owed	————
Total liabilities	————

Net Worth
  Total assets   ————
  Total liabilities   −   ————
  Net worth   ————

6
MAINTAINING A POSITIVE PERSONAL CASH FLOW

At least twice a year you should review your real cash flow, that is, the amount of money coming in and the amount going out. You may be surprised, because income and expenses can become somewhat blurred by the ready availability of credit card and bank credit. It's easy to run up bills that add up to more than you expect.

If you find that you actually have a negative cash flow—you're spending more than you're making—you should track your cash flow once a month and make the changes necessary to bring it in to line. You are not financially healthy, and you are in no position to invest, unless you have a positive cash flow.

The following chart provides a simple format for your use.

Cash Flow Analysis
Income   Amount
  Salary and commissions   _____
  Social Security   _____
Interest and dividends
  Profits from business enterprises   _____
  Miscellaneous fees and royalties   _____
  Alimony and/or child support   _____
          Total _____

Expenses   Amount
  Monthly living expenses:
    Household maintenance   _____
    Utilities   _____

Insurance _____
Transportation _____
Food _____
Clothing _____
Medical _____
Education _____
Personal, savings _____

Debt Obligations:
  Mortgage _____
  Principal and interest on bank debt _____
  Principal and interest on credit
    card debt _____
  Investment loans _____

Taxes:
  Federal _____
  State and Local _____
  Social security _____
  Real estate _____
              Total ═══════════════

Total your annual income and annual expenses and subtract the expense line from the income line. If there is a positive balance, you are in a position to invest.

If on the other hand, you have a negative cash flow, review each expense line and determine how much it can be cut back to bring your cash flow into line.

QUESTIONS AND ANSWERS

Where do female entrepreneurs come from?

Most women who start their own businesses come from middle class or lower middle class backgrounds. They are more likely to have gone to state schools than ivy league schools. They are, in fact, drawn from the same demographic group as male entrepreneurs.

Where do female entrepreneurs get their financing?

Women are most likely to launch their businesses on their own money or that of relatives. Only a small number go outside for bank loans or venture capital.

What kinds of businesses do women start?

The vast majority of businesses started by women are in the service sector rather than manufacturing.

How many women start businesses?

New business launches in the United States by women number about four times those started by men, and this difference is growing.

Where do women start their businesses?

Most women start their businesses at home.

Why do women start businesses?

Women start their own businesses for three main reasons. First, because of the multiplicity of women's roles, they start businesses to gain flexibility in their time schedules.

Second, women who feel they have gone as far as they

can in corporations (hitting the glass ceiling) start their own businesses.

Finally, women who were previously dependent on an employed husband or on the income and benefits of a retired husband and find themselves with neither start their own businesses.

What are the main personal characteristics of the female entrepreneur?

The female entrepreneur is most probably optimistic, disciplined, flexible, decisive, energetic, and good with people.

What will an executor do?

Your executor is responsible for administering your estate upon your death, according to your wishes. The executor will be required to pay outstanding bills, deal with insurance companies, and possibly sell real estate or even your own business. Your executor will contact your former employer to see to it that your heirs receive benefits due them. Finally, your executor will make sure that bequests, which you have made to various people, are properly carried out. If you have put funds in trust, the executor will handle the long-term payout rather than making a lump sum bequest to a beneficiary. The role of executor is difficult, tiring, and critical.

When should you start planning your retirement?

You should start planning your retirement as soon as you receive your first paycheck. It's good to develop the habit of saving at least five percent of your gross pay. This should be kept liquid until you amass enough to cover three months of living expenses. After that it should be invested conservatively for the long-range payout.

What is your investment risk tolerance?

To determine your risk tolerance, ask yourself how much of your life savings you are willing to risk on the outside chance of a higher return that that which you receive in conservative investments. If you are comfortable with only fifty percent of your investments in a conservative or even liquid state, then presumably you can stand the tension of knowing you could lose the whole other fifty percent.

If on the other hand, you have little or no risk tolerance, don't pretend you do. Invest everything conservatively so that you stay ahead of inflation and earn a decent return, one that you can depend on.

How much debt can you handle?

In difficult economic times, something close to zero is best (aside from your mortgage of course). Even in good times, it is not wise to get committed to anything beyond twenty percent of your net annual income.

Should you have a pre-nuptial or post-nuptial agreement?

Absolutely. Be realistic. Protect yourself. Avoid the possibility of expensive and drawn-out litigation at a later date.

How much insurance do you need?

Most probably, less life insurance than you have and more disability than you have. In all likelihood you don't have disability insurance at all. You should.

Before buying any insurance, carefully assess your real needs in terms of life, health, disability, and liability, and buy according to your real situation. Review your insurance coverage annually. As your lifestyle changes, so do your insurance needs.

Is real estate a sure thing?

No. In addition to economic ups and downs, there is the inescapable fact that housing built for the baby boomers does not have a ready market. The baby bust right behind the baby boom does not provide enough buyers for all of the baby boomers who want to sell their houses. Buy with great caution.

Can you hope to make a lifetime career in one company?

It is highly unlikely. Corporate America is undergoing enormous change—downsizing, merging, and repositioning. Many industries that have been the backbone of American employment are folding and being replaced by others which in many cases are far less stable.

What is financial planning?

Financial planning is the process whereby you seize control of your financial life and events as opposed to simply reacting to events after the fact. Financial planning deals in long-term and short-term goals.

If you run your own business and you live with someone, unmarried, does this other person have any rights to your business?

Possibly. This is a grey area, with little precedent. However, if this other person has contributed to the formation or even to the day-to-day running of your business, you could certainly have difficulty.

How much should you save?

Starting with your very first paycheck, you should save a minimum of five percent of your gross pay. If you do this for a lifetime, the impact of compound interest will be enormous and you will have a sizeable nest-egg upon retirement or when you need extra money for college tuition or possibly health care.

GLOSSARY

Annuities These are policies that, at maturity, pay either a lump sum or periodic payments to a retiree or another beneficiary of the policy.
Appreciation If an asset increases in value beyond its cost, it appreciates.
APR (Annual Percentage Rate) The total cost to you of any loan or credit.

Balance sheet The format you use to determine your net worth, listing all assets and all liabilities.
Bankruptcy There are two types of bankruptcy, voluntary and involuntary. *Voluntary Bankruptcy* is when you, the debtor, file in court. *Involuntary Bankruptcy* is when your creditors file in court asking that you be declared bankrupt.
Beneficiary The recipient of assets through enforcement of a trust, insurance policy, or will.
Broker That person who, for a commission or a fee, handles transactions between a buyer or seller, including real estate, insurance, stocks, and bonds.

Cash flow The difference between all of your income less all of your expenses.
Collateral Property, or a pledge to that property, turned over by you to a borrower to secure funds borrowed.
Compound interest An arrangement whereby interest is paid you on your principal as well as on previous interest paid.
Credit line The amount up to which a lending institution will permit you to borrow.
Credit rating A determination by credit reporting agencies regarding the amount and type of credit that you are able to carry.

Discretionary income This is your income after you have covered basic living expenses.
Diversification A method by which you spread your risk by using a variety of investments.
Dividends Payments to stockholders, set by the board of directors of the company, taking into consideration the earnings per share.

Employee Stock Option Plans (ESOPs) Programs open to employees to purchase their company's stock in an advantageous manner.
Equitable distribution An arrangement in a divorce, by court order, which distributes joint property acquired during a marriage . . . not necessarily equally.
Equity The value of an asset less any debt existing against it.
Executor The party responsible for disposition of your estate.

Inflation The increase in your cost of living, including price increases, which reduces the purchasing power of your dollars.

KEOGH Retirement plans for those who are self-employed.

Leverage Borrowed funds used to acquire an investment.
Limited partner An investor in business, liable only for the amount invested, without any operating authority.
Liquidity Any of your assets that are readily convertible to cash.

Origination fee The sum you must pay your bank for handling the administrative end of your mortgage.

Principal The original amount upon which interest is paid.

Profit sharing An employer plan that allows employees to share in the profits of the company.

Zero coupon bonds Bonds on which interest accumulates annually, but the interest is not paid out until maturity. However, unless these are part of an IRA or KEOGH you do have to pay taxes on interest annually.

INDEX

Accountant, 116
Advertising, 89–92
  case history, 101–102
Advisory board, 82–83
American Association of Minority Enterprise, 42
Attorney, 116–117
Awards of recognition, 89

Benefits, employee, 72
Billing, 55–56
Businesses:
  choosing type of, 13–14
  failures of, 7–8
  financing, 44–45
  location of, 29–30
  multiple, 61
  naming, 39
  ongoing financing, 48–49
  organization of, 36–38
  preparation for owner, 9–10
  selling, 99–100
  services v. products, 14
  time to start, 29
Business hours, 31
Business organization:
  going into with a friend, 37–38
  incorporation, 36
  partnership, 36–37
Business plan, 34–35
  sample: senior day care center, 111–113
Business travel, 64

Case histories, 101–103
Cash flow:
  billing and collection, 55–56
  personal emergency fund, 57
  positive, 122–123
  profits and, 56–57
  purchasing, 56
Cash requirements, 46–47
Chamber of Commerce, 8
Chief Financial Officer, 116
Child care costs, 93–94
Clerical staff, 119
COBRA, 85
Cold calls, 18
Collection, 55–56

Commercial banks, 45
Community work, 96
Company cars, 64–65
Company mailing list, 63
Competitors, 80–90
Consulting, 18–19
Corporate financing, 45
Corporate Legal Advisor, 116–117
Creative services agency, 90–91
Creative Services Director, 118–119
Credit line, 46–47
Credit rating, 47

Debt, 48–49
Direct mail test, 33
Disability insurance, 85
Discrimination, 59–60
Divorce, 94
Dress, 73

Emergency fund, 57
Equity, 48
Executor, 41
Existing business, purchase of, 21–22
Expenses, 34
Experts, using, 35

Family members, hiring, 75–76
Feasibility study, 32
  assessing, 109–110
  sample: senior day care center, 106–108
Female entrepreneur:
  characteristics of, 3
  corporate experience, 11–12
  discrimination and, 59–60
  entrepreneurial "type," 4–6
  problems of, 93–95
  sales experience, 11
  sources of, 1–2
Financial Planner, 116
Financing, 44–45
Financing terms, 22
Foreign businesses, 26–27
Former employer, servicing, 16–17
Franchises, 23–24
Freelancers, 70
Freelance sales, 15

Future, planning for, 28

Gender-related problems, 80–81
Glossary, 128–130
Goals, 97–98
Government contracts, 25, 44

Health insurance, 84–85

Income projections, 34
Incorporation, 36
Inflation, 53–54
Information, 42–43
Insurance:
  comparison shopping for, 86
  disability, 85
  health, 84–85
  key man, 86
  life, 85
  personal liability, 86
  property, 85–86
Interns, 77
Intrapreneuring, 15
Investors, 50

Job descriptions, 71–72
  examples of, 114–119

KEOGH plan, 52
Key man insurance, 86

Legal matters:
  licenses and permits, 40–41
  prior to launching business, 41
  zoning, 41
Licenses, 40
Life insurance, 85
Loans, 48–49
Loneliness, 95

Mailing list, 63
Management, outside, 78–79
Management ability, 7
Manufacturing, 14
Marketing, 89–92
Multiple businesses, 61

Naming company, 39
National Association of Women
  Business Owners, 42–43
Networking, 87–88
Net worth statement, 120–121
Net cash position, 50
Non-compete agreement, 17

Office:
  location of, 66–67
  owning space, 67–68
  subletting space, 67

Office decorum, 73
Office Manager, 114–115
Office of Women's Business
  Ownership (SBA), 42–43
Ongoing business, purchase of,
  21–22
Owner/President, 114
Owner role, 97–98

Partnership, 36–37
Permits, 40
Personal cash, 51–52
  maintaining positive cash flow,
  122–123
Personal liability insurance, 86
Personal net worth statement,
  120–121
Personnel:
  dress, 73
  employee benefits, 72
  job descriptions, 72–73
  office decorum, 73
  politics, 73–74
  problems with, 80–81
  promotions from within
    company, 72–73
  retirement age, 74
  salaries, 72
  training, 73
Politics, 73–74
Positive image, projection of,
  87–88
Problems, 93–95
Professional help, 82–83
Profits, 56–57
Promotions within company,
  72–73
Property insurance, 85–86
Psychiatry, case history, 101
Public relations, 16
  case history, 101
Publishing in your field, 87
Purchasing, 56

R & D, 16–17
Remarriage, 95
Retailing, 14
Retail space, 67
Retirement age, 74
Retirement plan, 52
Risk tolerance, 4–5

Salaries, 72
Sales experience, 11
Sales Manager, 115
Sales staff, 117–118
Savings, 51
  effect of inflation on, 53–54
Seasonal interns, 77

Secretary, 114–115, 119
Selling your company, 99–100
Service businesses, 14
Services, case history, 102–103
Side business expansion, 20
Small business expansion, 20
Small Business Administration, 8, 42, 45
Speaking in your field, 87
Staff, 69–70
Startup funding, 44–45
Subletting, 67
Summer interns, 77

Tax records, 58
Time management, 31
Training, employee, 73
Travel and entertainment, 64–65
Trusts, 41
Typists, 119

Under-capitalization, 7

Wholesaling, 14
Women's Forum, 42
Word processing, 119

Zoning, 41

BARRON'S BUSINESS KEYS Each "key" explains approximately 50 concepts and provides a glossary and index. Each book: Paperback, 160 pp., 4 3/16" x 7", $4.95, Can. $6.50. ISBN Prefix: 0-8120.

Keys for Women Starting or Owning a Business (4609-9)
Keys to Avoiding Probate and Reducing Estate Taxes (4668-4)
Keys to Business and Personal Financial Statements (4622-6)
Keys to Buying a Foreclosed Home (4765-6)
Keys to Buying a Franchise (4484-3)
Keys to Buying and Owning a Home (4251-4)
Keys to Buying and Selling a Business (4430-4)
Keys to Choosing a Financial Specialist (4545-9)
Keys to Conservative Investments (4762-1)
Keys to Estate Planning and Trusts, 2nd Edition (1710-2)
Keys to Financing a College Education, 2nd Edition (1634-3)
Keys to Improving Your Return on Investments (ROI) (4641-2)
Keys to Incorporating (3973-4)
Keys to Investing in Common Stocks (4291-3)
Keys to Investing in Corporate Bonds (4386-3)
Keys to Investing in Government Securities (4485-1)
Keys to Investing in International Stocks (4759-1)
Keys to Investing in Mutual Funds, 2nd Edition (4920-9)
Keys to Investing in Options and Futures (4481-9)
Keys to Investing in Real Estate, 2nd Edition (1435-9)
Keys to Investing in Your 401(K) (1873-7)
Keys to Managing Your Cash Flow (4755-9)
Keys to Mortgage Financing and Refinancing, 2nd Edition (1436-7)
Keys to Personal Financial Planning, 2nd Edition (1919-9)
Keys to Personal Insurance (4922-5)
Keys to Purchasing a Condo or a Co-op (4218-2)
Keys to Reading an Annual Report (3930-0)
Keys to Retirement Planning (4230-1)
Keys to Risks and Rewards of Penny Stocks (4300-6)
Keys to Saving Money on Income Taxes (4467-3)
Keys to Starting a Small Business (4487-8)
Keys to Surviving a Tax Audit (4513-0)
Keys to Understanding Bankruptcy, 2nd Edition (1817-6)
Keys to Understanding the Financial News, 2nd Edition (1694-7)
Keys to Understanding Securities (4229-8)
Keys to Women's Basic Professional Needs (4608-0)

Available at bookstores, or by mail from Barron's. Enclose check or money order for full amount plus sales tax where applicable and 10% for postage & handling (minimum charge $3.75, Can. $4.00) Prices subject to change without notice.

Barron's Educational Series, Inc. • 250 Wireless Blvd. Hauppauge, NY 11788 • Call toll-free: 1-800-645-3476 In Canada: Georgetown Book Warehouse 34 Armstrong Ave., Georgetown, Ont. L7G 4R9 Call toll-free: 1-800-247-7160

R 5/94

More selected BARRON'S titles:

DICTIONARY OF COMPUTER TERMS, 3rd EDITION
Douglas Downing and Michael Covington
Nearly 1,000 computer terms are clearly explained, and sample programs included. Paperback, $8.95, Canada $11.95/ISBN 4824-5, 288 pages

DICTIONARY OF FINANCE AND INVESTMENT TERMS,
3rd EDITION, *John Downs and Jordan Goodman*
Defines and explains over 3000 Wall Street terms for professionals, business students, and average investors.
Paperback $9.95, Canada $13.95/ISBN 4631-5, 544 pages

DICTIONARY OF INSURANCE TERMS, 2nd EDITION *Harvey W. Rubin*
Approximately 3000 insurance terms are defined as they relate to property, casualty, life, health, and other types of insurance.
Paperback, $9.95, Canada $13.95/ISBN 4632-3, 416 pages

DICTIONARY OF REAL ESTATE TERMS, 3rd EDITON
Jack P. Friedman, Jack C. Harris, and Bruce Lindeman
Defines over 1200 terms, with examples and illustrations. A key reference for anyone in real estate. Comprehensive and current.
Paperback, $10.95, Canada $13.95/ISBN 1434-0, 224 pages

ACCOUNTING HANDBOOK, *Joel G. Siegel and Jae K. Shim*
Provides accounting rules, guidelines, formulas and techniques etc. to help students and business professionals work out accounting problems. Hardcover: $29.95, Canada $38.95/ISBN 6176-4, 832 pages

REAL ESTATE HANDBOOK, 3rd EDITION
Jack P. Freidman and Jack C. Harris
A dictionary/reference for everyone in real estate. Defines over 1500 legal, financial, and architectural terms.
Hardcover, $29.95, Canada $39.95/ISBN 6330-9, 810 pages

HOW TO PREPARE FOR THE REAL ESTATE LICENSING
EXAMINATIONS-SALESPERSON AND BROKER, 4th EDITION
Bruce Lindeman and Jack P. Freidman
Reviews current exam topics and features updated model exams and supplemental exams, all with explained answers.
Paperback, $11.95, Canada $15.95/ISBN 4355-3, 340 pages

BARRON'S FINANCE AND INVESTMENT HANDBOOK,
3rd EDITION, *John Downes and Jordan Goodman*
This hard-working handbook of essential information defines more than 3000 key terms, and explores 30 basic investment opportunities. The investment information is thoroughly up-to-date. Hardcover $29.95, Canada $38.95/ISBN 6188-8, approx. 1152 pages

FINANCIAL TABLES FOR MONEY MANAGEMENT
Stephen S. Solomon, Dr. Clifford Marshall, Martin Pepper, Jack P. Freidman and Jack C. Harris
Pocket-sized handbooks of interest and investment rate tables used easily by average investors and mortgage holders. Paperback
Real Estate Loans, 2nd Ed., $6.95, Canada $8.95/ISBN 1618-1, 336 pages
Mortgage Payments, 2nd Ed., $5.95, Canada $7.95/ISBN 1386-7, 304 pages
Bonds, 2nd, $5.95, Canada $7.50/ISBN 4995-0, 256 pages
Comprehensive Annuities, $5.50, Canada $7.95/ISBN 2726-4, 160 pages
Canadian Mortgage Payments, 2nd Ed., Canada $8.95/ISBN 1617-3, 336 pages
Adjustable Rate Mortgages, 2nd Ed., $6.95, Canada $8.50/ISBN 1529-0, 288 pages

All prices are in U.S. and Canadian dollars and subject to change without notice. At your local bookseller, or order direct adding 10% postage (minimum charge $3.75, Canada $4.00), N.Y. residents add sales tax.   ISBN PREFIX 0-8120

Barron's Educational Series, Inc.
250 Wireless Boulevard, Hauppauge, NY 11788
Call toll-free: 1-800-645-3476
In Canada: Georgetown Book Warehoude
34 Armstrong Ave., Georgetown, Ontario L7G 4r9
Call toll-free: 1-800-247-7160

More selected BARRON'S titles:

DICTIONARY OF ACCOUNTING TERMS
Siegel and Shim
Nearly 2500 terms related to accounting are defined.
Paperback, $10.95, Can. $14.50 (3766-9)

DICTIONARY OF MARKETING TERMS
Imber and Toffler
Nearly 3000 terms used in the marketing and ad industry are defined.
Paperback, $11.95, Can. $15.95 (1783-8)

DICTIONARY OF BANKING TERMS
Fitch
Nearly 3000 terms related to banking, finance and money management.
Paperback, $10.95, Can. $14.50 (3946-7)

DICTIONARY OF BUSINESS TERMS, 2nd EDITION
Friedman, general editor
Over 6000 entries define business terms.
Paperback, $11.95, Can. $15.95 (1530-4)

BARRON'S BUSINESS REVIEW SERIES
These guides explain topics covered in a college level business course.
Each book: paperback
ACCOUNTING, 2nd EDITION. *Eisen.* $11.95,Can.$15.95 (4375 8)
BUSINESS LAW, 2nd EDITION. *Hardwicke and Emerson.* $11.95, Can. $15.95 (1385 9)
BUSINESS STATISTICS, 2nd EDITION. *Downing and Clark.* $11.95, Can. $15.95 (1384-0)
ECONOMICS, 2nd EDITION. *Wessels.* $11.95, Can. $15.95 (1392 1)
FINANCE, 2ndEDITION. *Groppelli and Nikbakht.* $11.95, Can. $15.95 (4373 1)
MANAGEMENT, 2nd EDITION. *Montana and Chanulv.* $11.95, Can. $15.95 (1549 5)
MARKETING, 2nd EDITION. *Sandhusen.* $11.95, Can. $15.95 (1548-7)
QUANTITATIVE METHODS. *Downing and Clark.* $10.95, Can. $14.95 (3947 5)

BARRON'S FOREIGN LANGUAGE BUSINESS DICTIONARIES
Six bilingual dictionaries translate about 3000 terms not found in most foreign phrasebooks:
Each book, paperback: $9.95, Can. $11.95
FRENCH FOR THE BUSINESS TRAVELER, ISBN 1768-4
GERMAN FOR THE BUSINESS TRAVELER, ISBN 1769-2
ITALIAN FOR THE BUSINESS TRAVELER, ISBN 1771-4
KOREAN FOR THE BUSINESS TRAVELER, ISBN 1772-1
RUSSIAN FOR THE BUSINESS TRAVELER, ISBN 1784-6
SPANISH FOR THE BUSINESS TRAVELER, ISBN 1773-0

All prices are in U.S. and Canadian dollars and subject to change without notice.
At your bookseller, or order direct adding 10% postage (rninumum charge $3.75, Canada $4.00) N.Y. residents add sales tax. ISBN PREFIX 0-8120

BARRON'S
Barron's Educational Series, Inc.
250 Wireless Boulevard, Hauppauge, NY 11788
Call toll-free: 1.800.645.3476
In Canada: Georgetown Book Warehouse
34 Armstrong Ave., Georgetown, Ontario L7G 4R9
Call toll-free: 1-800-247-7160